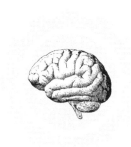

Master Your Mind

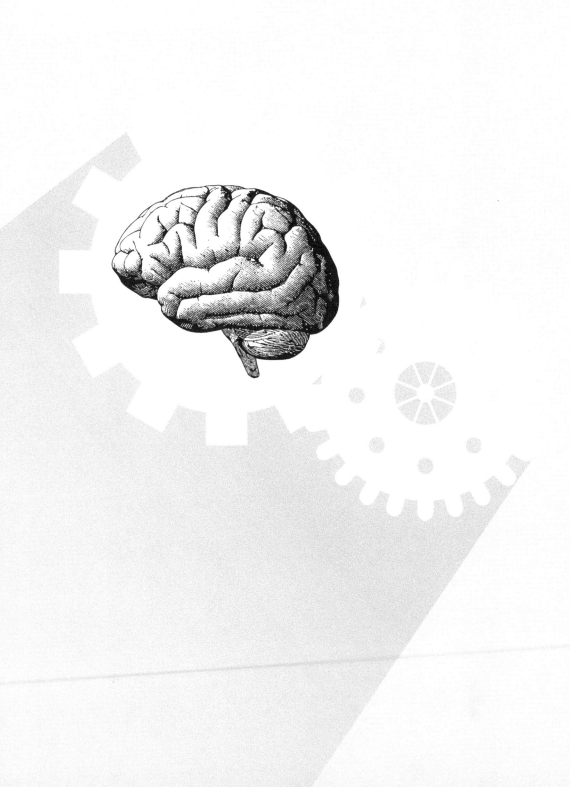

Master Your Mind

Critical-Thinking Exercises and Activities
to Boost Brain Power and Think Smarter

MARCEL DANESI, PhD

ROCKRIDGE
PRESS

For general information on our other products and services or to obtain technical support, please contact our Customer Care Department within the United States at (866) 744-2665, or outside the United States at (510) 253-0500.

Rockridge Press publishes its books in a variety of electronic and print formats. Some content that appears in print may not be available in electronic books, and vice versa.

Interior and Cover Designer: Linda Snorina
Art Producer: Samantha Ulban
Editor: Lori Tenny
Production Editor: Ruth Sakata Corley

All images used under license © Shutterstock

ISBN: Print 978-1-64739-326-7 | eBook 978-1-64739-327-4

R0

I would like to dedicate this book to my wonderful grandchildren, Alexander, Sarah, and Charlotte, who are all young critical thinkers most of the time. I also wish to dedicate it to all those who have been victimized by falsehoods, in the hope that they will find the intellectual tools in this book to shelter themselves from any future victimization brought about by dishonesty and duplicity.

Contents

Introduction

A while back, when my only child (a wonderful daughter) was a teenager, I faced challenges with her day in and day out—like any other parent, of course. I was especially frustrated by her nonchalance and indifference to my constant excoriations of her behavior. One day, I had a so-called epiphany! I realized that my approach was off-putting. I would say things like "When I was your age . . .," "You shouldn't do that, you know?" and so on. I realized that I was moralizing rather than reasoning with her. Gradually, I started engaging her in arguments and in dispassionate dialogues, focusing on ideas rather than on her behavior: "What message does your favorite band convey to someone like me?" "Did you read that article about drinking and driving? What do you think?"

The positive change in our relationship was almost instantaneous, and I came to realize the relevance of what the South African clergyman Desmond Tutu once said: "My father used to say, 'Don't raise your voice; improve your argument.'" I had discovered, in a phrase, the importance and power of *critical thinking*—the ability to evaluate something objectively, rather than emotionally, in order to form a judgment.

I am a professor of linguistics at the University of Toronto, and this experience changed my whole approach to teaching and led me to develop a keen interest in how the relationship between language and logic works, establish a course on puzzles and problem-solving at the university, and conduct research on this topic ever since. So here I am, ready to share my expertise with you, with a practical book that hopefully will not only help you improve relations with family members (if that is the case), but also sharpen your reasoning skills, alert you to falsehoods, and shield you against clever persuasive language—in short, a book that will help you develop the basic skills required for critical thinking. In an era of conspiracy theories, disinformation, and plain outright lies, these skills have become absolutely vital. The ability to see through the quagmire of disinformation throughout cyberspace and to evaluate complex subjects reflectively and objectively will put you in a better position to make reasonable choices in your daily life, from deciding what to buy to voting rationally to avoiding scams.

I planned this book to be as informative and enjoyable as possible for anyone. Educators looking for supplemental critical-thinking material will find this book provides digestible and engaging content. Unlike denser treatments of critical thinking, my goal is to get you involved in it through activities and real-life examples. Nonetheless, it will offer a comprehensive look at the major skills that underlie critical thinking in clear language.

How to Use This Book

Let me suggest a few ways to put this book to good use. You might, of course, find others.

When you read the skills described in each chapter and the examples given, think of similar experiences that you've had. Jot them down for future reflection. What would you do differently?

You will find real-world scenarios and case studies in each chapter that illustrate how critical-thinking skills are used—or abused, as the case may be. Consider what you might do if these topics, or similar ones, came up in conversation in your own life. What arguments would you make?

You will find exercises, activities, and puzzles throughout the chapters. They're designed to be challenging and illustrative at the same time, so work on them carefully before reading on. Take your time and check the answers (which can be found in the Answer Key section at the back of this book, organized by chapter) only after trying your best to figure out the solution. Keep in mind that in critical thinking, the particular answer given is only that—one particular answer. You might come up with others. Jot these down as well.

Have fun!

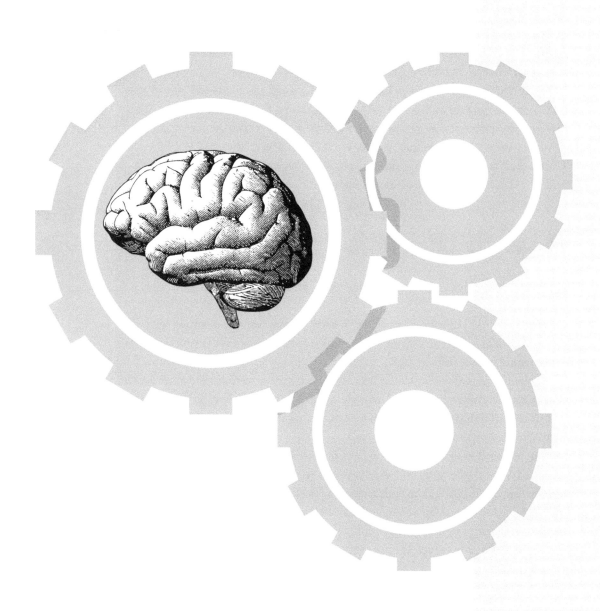

CHAPTER 1

Critical Thinking: The Basics

How many critical thinkers does it take to change a light bulb?

Consider the following situation: A light bulb in the ceiling has burned out. It's too high up for you to reach. How do you change it?

Possible solutions: Find a stool and stand on it. Ask a tall friend for help. Borrow a ladder from a neighbor. Do you have other suggestions?

Most of us could eventually resolve that problem. Why? Because we all have an innate sense of how things are in the world, and we use an instinctive form of reasoning to solve everyday problems. This is a key survival skill, and so ingrained that we're unaware how many times a day we use it. But awareness of the reasoning involved in our problem-solving is at the heart of *critical thinking*.

Critical thinking is much more than the ability to solve practical problems, like replacing a burned-out bulb. In this age of fake news, conspiracy theories, pseudoscience, and so on, being able to think critically immunizes us against bogus ideas (including the idea that immunization is bogus).

Maybe you've been taking your facility for critical thinking for granted, but no longer. It's time to hone this essential skill. To start, this chapter will describe exactly what critical thinking means, why it's important, how to use it, and what kinds of essential skills are involved in critical thinking. Before we move on to chapter 2, we'll also explore the top 10 traits of the critical thinker and close with a self-assessment quiz to test your own critical-thinking capacity.

Let someone else change that light bulb—you've got some reading to do!

What Is Critical Thinking?

Thinking is something we do all the time, consciously or unconsciously. But what *is* thinking? Good question! In fact, that has been a central question of philosophy and psychology since antiquity. So, very good question! Because thinking defies any viable definition—we need to use thinking itself to define what thinking is—psychologists divide thinking into specific categories, such as *cognition* and *memory*, among many others.

But even if we are not psychologists, we all intuitively know what's meant by the term "thinking," even if it's hard to articulate the definition. Let's consider another practical problem: Suppose it's raining heavily outdoors, but we urgently need to go out and buy something. Without thinking rationally, we might just go outside into the pouring rain. But this might entail negative consequences, such as getting soaking wet and developing a bad cold afterwards. So we *know*, inside of us, that it's best to dress appropriately, with a raincoat, and to take an umbrella. This knowledge comes from experience, of course, but the situation activates our present thinking about what to do.

Thinking, knowledge, and memory are intertwined, guiding our everyday acts. If we don't use our thinking caps, the consequences can range from trivial to literally "unthinkable." Now, *critical thinking* involves going a little deeper in our assessment of a situation. Let's go back to our example. This time, suppose that you forgot your rain-resistant apparel and umbrella at a friend's house. But you still need to go out. What to do? You analyze the viability of possible options: Order what you need through a website or over the phone; wait until the weather clears; run to and from the car to avoid getting too wet; text your friend and ask her to bring your rain gear over; and so on. Thinking rationally about options for tackling a specific problem falls under the rubric of *critical thinking*.

Critical thinking is really about making reasoned judgments, which means decoding hidden assumptions and their truth or falsity. It alerts us to *not* accept any information at face value, but rather to look below the surface, seeking evidence to support or refute a particular argument or course of action. A critical thinker is someone who asks questions such as these (politely, of course):

"How do you know that?"

"What evidence do you have to support what you're saying?"

"Are there alternatives to your point of view?"

These questions reveal several key traits about a critical thinker:

- **Being inquisitive**
- **Seeking evidence**
- **Adopting an attitude of healthy skepticism**
- **Being open, humbly, to new ideas or the ideas of others. That is, always accepting the possibility that we may be wrong when confronted with contradictory evidence.**

Who coined the term *critical thinking*? As far as I can tell, it was first used by American philosopher Max Black (1909–1988), in his 1946 book titled, aptly, *Critical Thinking*. He defined this quality as a blend of logic and imagination, claiming that we all possess it and can strengthen it by simple practice.

The example Black used to illustrate what he meant by this signature blend has come to be known as the "Mutilated Chessboard Problem." Can you figure it out? (Don't let the name alarm you; it's a nonviolent puzzle.)

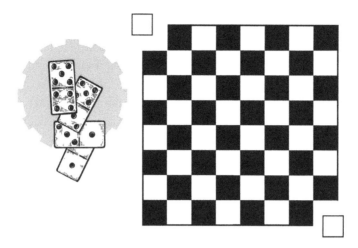

Remove two opposite corner squares of a typical chessboard. You are given a large number of dominoes. Each one is the size of two chessboard squares and is half black and half white. Is it possible to cover the entire chessboard with the dominoes, matching the black and white pattern exactly, with no dominoes hanging off the board? You cannot place the dominoes on top of each other, and they must lie flat.

The notion of critical thinking predates Black, even if it wasn't named that way. The American educator John Dewey (1859–1952) used the term *reflective thinking*, which he emphasized should guide our *actions*, not our habits of mind. Dewey's advice—to think reflectively before you act—is something that we should all take. You will have a chance to engage in such thinking throughout this book.

So with that in mind, we can identify three key skills for critical thinking:

1. **Making informed decisions.** Recall the vignette about going out in the rain. It illustrates that to resolve situations, we gather information that will help us decide what to do, whether we're aware of it or not.

2. **Considering options.** Recall the light bulb problem: To resolve the situation, we considered various courses of action, weighing each to choose the optimal one.

3. **Analyzing the situation methodically.** The "Mutilated Chessboard Problem" shows how examining a situation and looking for hidden patterns can resolve what might seem like an intractable problem.

Critical thinking is thinking about your thinking while you're thinking in order to make your thinking better.

—Richard W. Paul

ACTIVATE THOSE CRITICAL-THINKING SKILLS!

Which critical-thinking skill should be used in the following situations? Consider each scenario and decide whether it would be best to tackle it by making an informed decision, considering options, or analyzing the situation methodically.

1. **Coffee stop.** You're scrolling through your social media feed, and a link takes you to an article titled "Wow, Drinking Coffee Is Bad for You, Says a Coffee Scientist." You love coffee, but you don't like things that are bad for you. How can you resolve this?

_____

_____

_____

_____

2. **Apt advice?** You've decided you want to create an online dating app for people with dogs, called Hounder. A friend tells you that developing an app is an expensive, complicated, time-consuming process. You want to go forward with your project. What's the next step?

_____

_____

_____

_____

3. **Help wanted!** You get an email from a friend you haven't seen for a while. Her message states that she is in desperation and seeking help from you. She says she was on vacation in the Caribbean and ran into trouble with the police. She needs money for bail. She begs you to help her out "in remembrance of the good friend time we had" by clicking a link and entering your bank information. What's the best strategy to determine your response?

Let's challenge your analytical skills with a classic puzzle. If you analyze the information methodically, you should be able to come up with the solution.

You are given six billiard balls that look and feel exactly alike, but one of them weighs less than the others. Since you can't tell the difference, you can use a balance scale—the kind with a seesaw mechanism and a pan on each side—to identify the lighter ball. But you're only allowed to use the scale twice. How do you do it?

Why Is Critical Thinking Important?

Using critical thinking can be compared to solving jigsaw puzzles—it involves reviewing pieces of information and seeing how they fit, or don't, without overlooking any pieces or trying to force a connection that isn't there. We use both imagination, envisioning which pieces might fit together, and logic, methodically testing combinations and tracking the results.

These days, there's no shortage of puzzles to solve. We live in an age filled with misinformation, contradictions, and mixed messages. Sound bites, memes, and viral videos bombard us on a daily basis, clouding our ability to decide what is meaningful. Critical thinking is now more critical than it ever was. Thinking critically shields us from unreflectively accepting whatever information is presented to us, including the following two common sources of misinformation:

Ignorant certainty. The false belief that there are correct answers to all questions. The answers to everyday questions are rarely straightforward. Should you go to the store in the pouring rain without a raincoat or umbrella? No, if you're coming down with a cold and you can go tomorrow when it's sunny out. Yes, if you don't mind getting drenched and need to pick up prescription medication before the pharmacy closes.

Naive relativism. The false belief that there is no truth and that all facts are equal. If a music critic pans an album that you enjoy, you might argue that his opinion is no truer than yours. But you certainly would not want your family doctor to think this way!

Everyone should make critical thinking the cornerstone of their personal and professional life. Here's what critical thinking can do for you:

Enhance your ability to analyze. In a critical-thinking framework, *analysis* means examining something in detail in order to reach a plausible conclusion. This was important for figuring out the chessboard and billiard ball puzzles. It's what a doctor does when you show up to your appointment with a cough, fever, and sore throat: the doctor will analyze the symptoms on the basis of their expertise, make a diagnosis based on the possibility that the symptoms indicate a certain ailment, and then tell you what actions to undertake.

Promote clearer understanding. This is a by-product of the previous skill. Methodical analysis of a situation leads to a better understanding of that situation. Suppose you're a school counselor trying to help teenagers understand why drug use might hurt them. Instead of simply issuing warnings, you can lead them to a clearer understanding by inviting them to analyze the situation along with you. You might ask why they think using drugs is safe, discuss their responses, and provide facts that speak to their beliefs. This analysis will lead them to a clearer understanding of the situation that will serve them better than lectures or scare tactics.

Instill patience. Making a practice of seeking the right information and analyzing the situation gets us used to taking the time necessary to find the best solution. That's a much better approach than rushing to judgment, especially with high-stakes decisions like moving to a new home or pursuing a different career path.

Spark creativity. Critical thinking impels us to develop innovative solutions, a phenomenon called *lateral thinking*. That term was introduced by Edward de Bono, a Maltese-born British psychologist who cites the famous story of King Solomon as an example: Two women came before Solomon, both claiming to be the mother of the same child. Solomon proposed splitting the infant in two, to give each woman half as a fair solution. Not the expected answer! But he knew full well that the real mother would give up her child to the other woman to spare its life. Which is exactly how Solomon was able to identify the real mom. Sometimes critical thinking reveals a path forward that might have been overlooked.

Prevent mistakes. Acting without critical thinking can leave us in the rain without an umbrella, spending a fortune to create an app that's doomed to fail, or giving up our bank account information to an email scammer pretending to be our friend. Mistakes are inevitable in life, and reward often requires taking a risk. But the use of critical thinking can at the very least minimize our missteps.

Take you beyond the obvious. Habitual thinking sometimes leads us to make poor decisions, because doing the exact same thing every time leaves us unprepared for change. Critical thinking, on the other hand, reveals hidden information that prompts us to look beyond the obvious for a solution. This is what detectives, real and fictional, have always done: think beyond the evidence at hand to consider all the facts and create an overall picture of a crime. It worked for Sherlock Holmes, and it will work for you.

The Brain is wider than the Sky.

—Emily Dickinson

When to Use Critical Thinking

It might be more appropriate to ask "When *shouldn't* we use critical thinking?" Analyzing, evaluating, being open-minded, and all the other qualities of a critical thinker can be applied to more situations than you might expect. Here are a few examples.

PERSONAL LIFE

Consuming online content such as news stories, blog posts, and social media posts. Digital media have greatly expanded our ability to communicate, access all kinds of information, and stay informed. But we can't count on the information coming our way to be filtered for quality or accuracy. And our instantaneous access makes it easy to absorb everything mindlessly. (At least with a newspaper, you might have a thoughtful moment while turning to the sports page.) Critical thinking may be our best defense against the fake information, biased claims, and conspiracy theories that permeate the internet.

Voting. Elections are game changers, so voting is not to be taken lightly. Fake news, ingenious hacking schemes, and other threats require us to muster critical thinking to be sure that our vote is well placed and not influenced by false claims or counterfeit data.

Sitting on a jury. Jury duty is an important responsibility, since a jury's decision can change someone's life permanently. Critical thinking will tell us whether the bits and pieces of evidence fit together, independent of passionate counter-arguments made by the attorneys.

Purchasing a car, house, or other big-ticket item. With critical thinking to help us analyze the situation logically, we put our impulsiveness in check and avoid overspending.

Planning a budget. A personal or household budget is key for managing our finances, but only if it logically takes into account our true needs—health insurance, yes; video games, not so much—and is realistic for our income and expenses.

Assembling or fixing things. When your cable reception goes out or your car starts making an odd noise, what should you do? If a basement pipe is leaking and there's a hole in the roof, which should be repaired first? How much troubleshooting can you do on your own before you need to call a professional? Critical thinking helps you navigate these minor or major crises . . . if you're honest in your analysis. Do you really know how to replace a roof shingle, or are you likely to slide off and end up in the emergency room?

PROFESSIONAL LIFE

Career advancement. Many careers today require workers with good critical-thinking skills. These include the ability to distinguish between useless and relevant information, organize work schedules, prioritize tasks, set up and run sales and marketing reports, plan advertising and promotional campaigns, evaluate employee performances, and predict industry trends and buying patterns. An employee who can attack a novel problem and solve it will be welcome in any workplace.

Analyzing metrics. Web traffic analytics, sales reports, profit-and-loss statements, economic indicators . . . statistics and facts are everywhere in the business world. But critical thinking is required to make sense of the numbers.

Setting budget goals. Planning where and how much to spend is no easy task, but it's central to any business operation, big or small. Without critical thinking, a spending budget is a roll of the dice.

Hiring the right candidate. Job interviews often involve questions designed to test a candidate's critical-thinking skills. As we shall see later in this book, the thinking patterns used for logical analysis will come in handy in such a situation.

Project management. Managing a project on time and within budget, not to mention dealing with obstacles along the way, is impossible to do without the ability to think critically.

Expansion and growth. Whether it's a single small department or an entire corporation, growing a business requires strategic planning, organizing, and analyzing information, all of which are critical-thinking skills.

Developing the Skill Set

You'll learn all about these critical-thinking traits and how to develop them as you work through the exercises and read the case studies in the coming chapters of this book.

Analysis. This is a primary skill that underlies most of the other critical-thinking skills. A big part of it is always questioning the truth of something. Let's say your aunt takes a certain vitamin every day. Then, on the one day she forgets to take it, she becomes ill. She insists that you will also become ill if you don't take the vitamin. Do you accept her advice? The analytic approach would be to investigate the effects of the vitamin, doing research to see whether your aunt's claim is plausible.

Interpretation. Collecting information is one thing; the ability to interpret it objectively is another. If you assume that your aunt became ill because she didn't take her vitamin, are you correctly interpreting the course of events? You may need to check multiple credible sources of information to be sure.

Inference. This means reaching a conclusion on the basis of some form of reasoning, supported by reliable information and evidence. As you will see in a subsequent chapter, a correct inference moves from true premises to logical outcomes or conclusions. Our tendency is to jump to conclusions from insufficient or faulty premises; critical thinking guards us against this tendency.

Evaluation. Sometimes making judgments or decisions rationally involves evaluating the evidence and deciding whether the information we have at hand is truly of value. In the above example, our aunt's experience isn't evidence enough to infer that the vitamin will avert sickness, so we'd need to seek out more data to make a judgment.

Explanation. After compiling relevant information and evaluating it through analysis, interpretation, and logical inferences, you should always seek an explanation: "What does this mean?" "Is there a general principle at work here?" "What did I learn that will apply to similar situations in the future?"

Problem-solving. What is a problem? That simple question is one of the most elusive questions of mathematics, philosophy, and psychology! But we know intuitively what a problem looks like; most of us have more of them than we'd like. In the context of critical thinking, what we call a problem typically comes in the form of a question that requires a definite answer. For example, rank the following means of transportation in order from slowest to fastest: (1) sailing, (2) riding a bike, (3) flying, (4) walking, (5) driving. The solution is: 4-2-5-1-3. That exercise exemplifies what a problem is about—organizing facts in a way that leads to a solution. The ability to do that is a key critical-thinking skill.

Decision-making. The overriding objective of most critical thinking is not only to solve a problem but to use that solution to make a correct decision. Analysis, evaluation, and other critical-thinking skills guard us against making a potentially wrong or inconvenient decision and enhance the likelihood of making a correct one.

TOP 10 TRAITS OF A CRITICAL THINKER

What makes someone a critical thinker? Watch for these characteristics.

1. **Open-mindedness.** Critical thinkers are always inclined to listen to others and to consider new ideas in a nonprejudicial way. This includes considering the ideas of an opponent.

2. **Decisiveness.** Problems and crises crop up all the time. Critical thinkers will tend to be decisive about what to do about them, with confidence that considering all options, analyzing the situation methodically, and making an informed decision will lead to an effective solution.

3. **Creativity.** Critical thinking can be defined as a blend of logic and imagination that enhances our ability to solve problems. Critical thinkers can use their imagination to consider previous experiences and knowledge and see where that leads.

4. **Objectivity.** Looking at a situation independently of one's previous beliefs or acquired knowledge is a powerful shield against making wrong assumptions. Critical thinkers know that just because we've always done something a certain way, that doesn't mean there's not a better way to do it.

5. **Awareness.** Critical thinkers value being informed about all possibilities involved in a situation, whether it's a tried-and-true solution or a so-crazy-it-just-might-work alternative.

6. **Perseverance.** Don't give up! Often the effort to solve a seemingly intractable problem will itself provide new information and knowledge, opening up new possibilities and new ways of thinking.

7. **Language acumen.** Critical thinkers are aware that language can deceive us, which is why we'll be taking a close look at rhetoric, or the art of persuasion in speech or writing, later in this book. As George Orwell wrote: "The great enemy of clear language is insincerity."

8. **Using experience constructively.** Successful problem-solving includes the ability to link a present problem to one that was solved previously and to apply what was learned from the previous problem to the new problem.

9. **Curiosity.** Curiosity killed the cat, as the proverb warns, but the cliché refers to random curiosity. In critical thinking, curiosity is always guided by reason. Critical thinkers possess a strong desire to examine all kinds of situations to understand them and see what can be gleaned from them.

10. **Skepticism.** Doubting the validity of something until we examine its logic, or its basis in actual verifiable facts, is more important than ever when we're surrounded by so much misinformation.

A CRITICAL-THINKING SELF-ASSESSMENT QUIZ

The following quiz will allow you to test your own critical-thinking skills—that is, it will help you determine for yourself how you currently view your own ability to employ the techniques necessary to think critically.

1. You are told that a new influenza vaccine will completely immunize you against the flu. You don't have any particular knowledge on the subject. How do you respond?

    A) *Accept this as fact and go get the vaccine.*

    B) *Ignore it and don't get vaccinated.*

    C) *Ask someone in the know, like your physician, or check with an authoritative source, then make your decision.*

2. As you know, or at least have learned from living in society or watching cartoons, it's said that cats and dogs are inimical to each other. Your friend Jack's aunt has a cute Persian cat and a rambunctious bulldog. You run into Jack on his way to visit his aunt for the first time since she acquired her pets. He tells you, "I know what I will find there."

    Given what Jack has learned from living in the same world as you, what scenario is he predicting? Will he be right?

3. The following puzzle was devised by the American puzzle maker Sam Loyd (1841–1911). It is a classic example of the imaginative thinking that's involved in tricky problem-solving:

    Uncle Reuben never married. Yesterday he came to town to visit his sister, Mary Ann. As they were strolling along a street, they reached a hospital. "Before we move on," Reuben said to his sister, "I want to stop for a sec and ask about my sick nephew who is in the hospital." "No problem," replied Mary Ann, "and since I do not have any sick nephew to worry about, I will continue on home and meet up with you later." What relation did the nephew have to Mary Ann?

4. You get into a heated argument with a friend about climate change. He becomes quite irate and says, "Nobody has proven to me there is climate change. There is no such thing!" Which response is most characteristic of a critical thinker?

    A) *Let's change the subject; you're not thinking logically. Also, there's cake over there.*

    B) *Why don't you take a look at some information I'll send you, and we'll revisit this?*

    C) *There's plenty of proof, but you choose not to see it.*

5. After your friend takes your advice and checks out different views of climate change, he comes back to you and says, "Climate change might be true for you and your liberal friends, but it still is not for me." How do you analyze his statement?

   A) *Your friend's beliefs are stronger than logic or evidence.*

   B) *Your friend can be convinced if you keep politics out of it.*

   C) *Your friend has drawn a wrong conclusion.*

6. You receive an email about an upcoming election from a source that seems legitimate. It provides damaging information about a specific politician, implying that you should use it to make your decision about whom to vote for. Which critical-thinking quality is most useful in processing or evaluating the information?

   A) *Skepticism*

   B) *Objectivity*

   C) *Curiosity*

7. You receive an internal email stating that the company you work for is undergoing financial problems, and streamlining will take place shortly. Before deciding whether to seek a job elsewhere, which of the following would you do?

   A) *Reply with questions about the reasons for the problems.*

   B) *Consult with your colleagues about the situation.*

   C) *Search for outside evaluations about how the company is faring and how the economy and other factors are affecting things.*

   D) *All of the above.*

8. You are given a budgeting problem to solve. The current budget allocations seem to lead to a deficit, and you're asked specifically to come up with a solution that will keep things in the black. You try every approach you know, but no matter how many times you attempt to resolve the problem, you cannot avoid the deficit. What should you do next?

   A) *Be honest and tell your boss that the problem is beyond your ability.*

   B) *Keep trying. Eventually some solution will come to you.*

   C) *Seek outside information about how a similar situation was resolved elsewhere.*

9. A trusted friend tells you, a migraine sufferer, that you should take a new miracle drug for migraine headaches. How would you respond?

   A) *Try the medication on the word of your friend.*

   B) *Ignore her advice and stick with treatments you know.*

   C) *Look up reputable sources to confirm or disconfirm your friend's assertion.*

   D) *Set up your own self-styled clinical trial with members of your migraine support group, getting others to try the drug and then collecting and analyzing the results.*

10. For your last question, let's practice critical thinking with a bit of fun with this classic problem. It's attributed to the medieval scholar Alcuin of York (735–804 CE). It goes like this:

    A farmer reaches a riverbank with a goat, a wolf, and a head of cabbage. He finds a boat that's only big enough to hold himself and one of the items. He knows that if left together, the goat will eat the cabbage, and the wolf will eat the goat. How does he get everything, including himself, across the river so he can continue his journey? To answer, you'll have to analyze the information carefully.

Key Takeaways: CHAPTER 1

Thinking is the hardest work there is, which is probably the reason so few engage in it.

—Henry Ford

Let's sum up the main points to take away from this chapter.

1. Critical thinking is something we all possess but may not use consistently, especially since false beliefs can cloud our minds.

2. Critical thinking is about making reasoned judgments, which means decoding hidden assumptions and their truth or falsity.

3. Most thinking is habitual or automatic. When we think critically, we can grasp a situation better by deliberately employing intellectual tools to reach more accurate conclusions.

4. In today's digitally driven world, there is nothing more critical than critical thinking. Edward de Bono sums it up best: "There's a danger in the internet and social media. The notion that information is enough, that more and more information is enough, that you don't have to think, you just have to get more information—gets very dangerous."

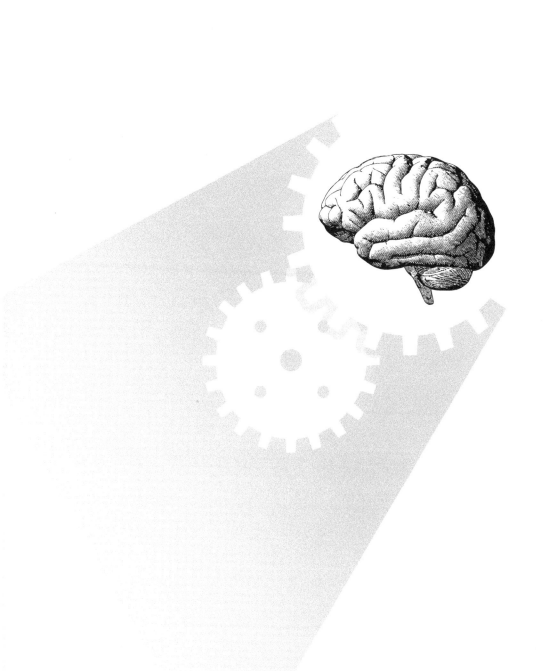

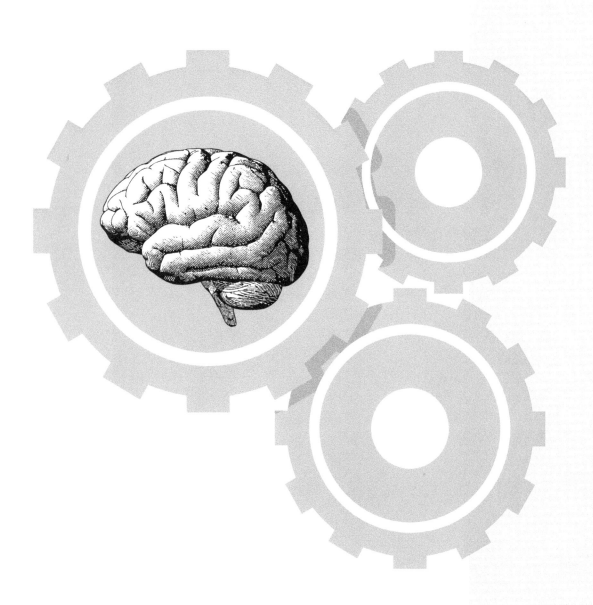

CHAPTER 2

The Art of Reasoning

Since the dawn of history, humans have been arguing about the tug-of-war within us: between logic and emotion, reasoning and believing, and acting purposefully and reacting mindlessly. The conflict continues to be expressed in modern pop culture. In the sci-fi franchise *Star Trek*, the character known as Mr. Spock is constantly pitting his use of logic against the emotional reactions of the human beings around him. Half human himself, Spock occasionally gives in to his own emotional side. But for the most part, he's a master of the *art of reasoning*—the primary art on which critical thinking is based.

Similarly, on the sitcom *The Big Bang Theory*, the character Sheldon— whose hero is, not surprisingly, Mr. Spock—is always extolling and illustrating the art of reasoning. But he, too, concedes to his heart, eventually falling in love with Amy, his female counterpart.

The critical thinker understands this mental and emotional contest and how it unfolds in every word and action. The goal is not to extinguish emotions, as Spock's Vulcan brethren would have it. Rather, the art of reasoning grants the ability to distinguish logic-based arguments from emotional ones, so we can take appropriate action in response.

Our examination of this subject will take us through these components of the art of reasoning:

- The differences between assertions, arguments, and non-arguments, and how each of them unfolds

- How sound and unsound arguments are constructed

- How two types of reasoning, deduction and induction, manifest themselves in everyday discourse and actions

- The differences between explanations, theories, and hypotheses

Reasonably Speaking

The great Greek philosopher and teacher Socrates taught that everyone is born with the ability to figure things out by reasoning about them. As his pupil Plato recounts in his text *Meno*, Socrates led an unschooled slave to grasp a mathematical principle by getting him to reflect on it systematically. However, Socrates also knew that the same type of reasoning can be used to deceive or even harm someone. As he himself remarked, "False words are not only evil in themselves, but they infect the soul with evil." His warning applies especially today, in an age of fake news, conspiracy theories, and the like. So let his wise words guide us through the art of reasoning.

ASSERTIONS

As an example of what Socrates is talking about, let's consider the argument of Susan Sontag (1933–2004), who in her brilliant 1978 book *Illness as Metaphor* stated that the words we use can be dangerous, literally, to people's health. Expressions and assertions such as "I wonder what he did to deserve cancer?" or "She can only blame herself for her breast cancer" place the blame for cancer on the victim, making them as harmful to a patient's health as the disease itself.

Stating something confidently with implied authority is an *assertion*. We make assertions all the time, often without support or justification that they are valid or true. We do this for a variety of reasons—for expediency, to declare certain beliefs, or simply to get a personal viewpoint across. Here are two more examples on the subject of health and illness.

"He must have been a heavy smoker; otherwise he couldn't have gotten lung cancer."

"This is what happens when your diet is unhealthy—you get diabetes."

Both statements reveal how unsupported assertions typically manifest themselves— as opinions that lack any evidence that they are true or, at the very least, are only applicable in specific cases. They link certain diseases judgmentally with lifestyle. This linkage may be valid in general, but its specific applications may not be—for instance, lung cancer can be contracted from secondhand smoke and diabetes from genetics. Whatever the truth, these assertions blame the victim, which, as Sontag knew, is as injurious as the disease itself. And these assertions are presented as self-evident generalizations and thus beyond reproach.

Unjustified assertions can be dangerous in many ways. In politics, for example, they are often deployed strategically as principles to keep people of the same political stripe together, blocking valid counterarguments. These are colloquially known as "talking points," preestablished speech formulas that are repeated over and over so that they can remain believable and stable through the repetition itself. We must always be wary of such generalizations.

ARGUMENTS

Assertions are often presented in the form of *arguments*, which are statements that present something in such a way that they imply a specific logical conclusion. Now, the problem may be that an argument may be valid but not true; that is, it may hold together logically, but it may not accurately describe reality. Validity and truth are not the same thing. Indeed, arguments are used to distort reality all the time.

So, how do we guard against false arguments? As Socrates himself taught, we must grasp how arguments work logically, so that we can test and evaluate their truth or validity. Arguments are based on three logical processes—*deduction, induction*, and *plausible inference*. The first involves deriving conclusions from given premises; the second entails reaching a conclusion on the basis of repeating facts or patterns; and the last draws a conclusion on the basis of informed guessing.

In all arguments, the goal is to lead someone to a conclusion from certain assertions, even if that conclusion doesn't reflect the truth of the real world. In an argument, it's the reasoning used that leads us to the conclusion. This is why we must always be cautious or circumspect about any argument. To see what this means, let's consider a typical courtroom cross-examination, the objective of which is to trap the accused into admitting something.

Prosecutor: Did you run into the murder victim on the day she disappeared?

Accused: No, I absolutely did not.

Prosecutor: Really? So why did you tell the police that you ran into her on the bus that morning?

Accused: Did I say that?

Prosecutor: Yes, you sure did. Can you explain the anomaly?

The prosecutor's argument was to connect the accused's assertion, "No, I absolutely did not," to something he said previously, namely his admission to the police that he met the victim on the day of the crime. This implies a contradiction and leads to a conclusion that the accused is lying. Or at least the prosecuting attorney hopes the jury will reach that conclusion.

Based on the premise that the accused made two contradictory statements, the logical conclusion is that one of them is a lie. And this will cast doubt on the innocence of the accused. But the truth may be something else entirely—for instance, the accused may be confused about the time and situation of the encounter. Or perhaps the prosecutor is lying and the accused never said that he met the victim. (One hopes the defense attorney will object.) Clearly, arguments that are stitched together logically can be used to entrap us or deceive us. Of course, they are also used for truth-seeking. Perhaps the accused is guilty and did lie about meeting the victim, and the prosecutor's argumentation will lead to a conviction.

NONARGUMENTS

Some arguments should instantly be disregarded because they either make no sense or are patently invalid. These are, in fact, nonarguments masquerading as the real thing. They have the form of a legitimate argument and thus may appear believable, but below the surface their objective is to persuade not with logic but by trickery. Common methods of making a nonargument include:

Connecting premises and conclusions on the basis of belief. "The winter weather is warmer than usual; obviously, climate change works for the better." This utilizes an unfounded belief that warmer weather in one instance indicates a general trend.

Giving a warning from a false premise. "Do not vote for him; one should never trust short people." This is clearly an absurd nonargument. However, it cannot be ignored, since false premises are not always as conspicuous as this one. For example, "Don't adopt this dog; that breed is always vicious."

Explanations that have no basis in fact. "Vegetables are not good for us, because they grow in the ground." Conjunctions such as *because* and *since* are often used to link premises with absurd conclusions. As nonsensical as these statements may be, the linguistic structure can be persuasive enough for them to fly under the radar. Beware!

Backing up a nonargument with irrelevant illustrations. "You don't get my point? Well, let me illustrate it further." We have all heard someone say this. If the point is valid, the illustration might be helpful, but if it is not, then it will be irrelevant.

Connecting premises and a conclusion on a certain condition. "If he's a white supremacist, I'm a frog." Again, this might seem absurd, but in some contexts this approach has persuasive force, given its ironic intent. In fact, irony has a way of duping us into accepting nonarguments as valid. An ironic statement seems to say, "This is so obviously true that I don't need to seriously defend it."

ANATOMY OF AN ARGUMENT

Now that we've seen what an argument is—an attempt to lead someone to a conclusion—and examined what it isn't, it's time to take a closer look.

Greek philosopher Aristotle (384–322 BCE) provided us with the first model of how arguments work. He called it the *syllogism*. This is a three-part structure that shows how an argument leads us to reach a conclusion by linking one premise to another. For example:

Major premise: Mammals are warm-blooded.

Minor premise: Cats are mammals.

Conclusion: Therefore cats are warm-blooded.

The *major premise* is the part of the syllogism to which we must always devote our full critical attention. It is a general statement, or assertion, that can be true or not. In the case above, it is true. But if it's not true, then the conclusion it leads to is suspect, even though it's reached logically.

The *minor premise* is a statement about something specific that connects it to the major premise. In this example, it is also true. When the major and minor premises are linked, they lead logically to the conclusion. If the minor premise is not true ("Frogs are mammals."), the persuasive power of the linkage itself may lead us to accept a conclusion that is untrue ("Frogs are warm-blooded.") or even dangerous ("Apples are safe to eat; rocks are apples; therefore rocks are safe to eat.").

As we saw with the cross-examination vignette above, as long as something seems logical, we are inclined to accept its conclusions as being true. But this is not necessarily so. Since antiquity, logicians have discussed and warned us against strategies designed to lead us to wrong conclusions. Here are five common ones—some of which will be revisited in subsequent chapters of this book:

Unconfirmable conclusion. This is a conclusion that cannot be confirmed because there is no empirical way to check whether it is true or even what it actually means: "She is evil; do not listen to her." What does it mean to be *evil*? How do we find out? Well, we cannot. We can only accept (or not) the speaker's conclusion as true.

Untenable conclusion. This is a statement that conceals a conclusion derived from an untenable premise: "If you got arrested, don't complain; you must have something to hide." The premise that anyone who is arrested must be guilty cannot be held as tenable; an arrest could have been an error or based on an unfounded accusation.

Specious cause and effect. This is a statement that connects two events as directly related with no proof whatsoever of the connection. A classic example comes from the 1999 Columbine High School mass shooting. The two killers listened to the music of Marilyn Manson. Many believed this to be a cause of their violence. But evidence showed the truth to be more complex. This type of argument aims to reduce something that is complicated to a simple explanation.

Claiming an anonymous authoritative source. This is a statement which asserts that "they say" or "studies confirm" that something is the way it is, with no direct specifics as to the authoritative sources. For example, "They say that climate change is a hoax" and "Studies show that coffee is bad for you." Who are *they*? Which *studies* are referenced?

Popular beliefs. Some declarations employ language based on commonly held stereotypes and metaphors that assert something as true even when it isn't: "Everyone knows illegal immigrants join gangs and do drugs." This may be a common viewpoint, but examining real data may suggest the opposite.

———————————————

An ignorance of means may minister to greatness, but an ignorance of aims makes it impossible to be great at all.

—Elizabeth Barrett Browning

CASE STUDY: *THE DREYFUS AFFAIR*

A classic case of what happens when facts are manipulated and assertions are made about someone with no real evidence to back them up is the so-called Dreyfus Affair. In 1894, a French army officer named Alfred Dreyfus (1859–1935) was falsely accused of providing military secrets to Germany. His trial, conviction, and imprisonment sparked a major political crisis in France. The miscarriage of justice was attributed to the fact that Dreyfus was Jewish. So no matter what evidence was brought forward in his defense and how logical the arguments in his favor were, reason yielded to false beliefs and hidden prejudices. Anti-Semitic groups used the Dreyfus trial to stir up racial hatred. As was later discovered, the incriminating evidence was fabricated by an army major, Charles Esterhazy. Dreyfus was given a second trial in 1899, but he was again declared guilty of treason, despite evidence of his innocence. He was finally exonerated in 1906.

The Dreyfus Affair is just one example of how people are susceptible and even vulnerable to false beliefs and prejudices, and how these can be stoked by clever arguments (or nonarguments) based on false premises, designed to manipulate the mind. The only true antidote is to constantly challenge perceived opinions and beliefs—to be certain that the major and minor premises of any argument are true before accepting any conclusions. Similar events have occurred throughout history, suggesting that reason is often at risk in the face of belief systems. False conspiracies such as the one perpetrated by Esterhazy are particularly destructive because they tap into prejudices that may be hidden unconsciously, stoking resentment against a targeted group. The great political theorist Hannah Arendt (1906–1975) once stated that the reason conspiracies and lies have such deleterious effects is "not that you believe the lies, but rather that nobody believes anything any longer."

CHECK THE CONCLUSION

It's time to play Doctor Aristotle and dissect some arguments!
Each of the following statements presents something as being necessarily so.
Identify the faulty reasoning behind each one.

1. "Yesterday I saw my boss driving a Ferrari. Well, anyone who drives such a car must be rich."

2. "Good workers always get to work on time. Mary never comes in late. She must be a good worker."

3. "Every time someone is at our door, our cat Hazel starts purring. Hazel is purring now, so there must be someone at the door."

4. "My father suffered a heart attack a few years ago, as did his mother and my grandmother when she was younger. It is inevitable that I will also have a heart attack."

_____

_____

_____

ASSESS THE ASSERTION

Match each statement to its most accurate description.

Statements:

1. "Research published in the _New England Journal of Medicine_ links sugar to many diseases. We should be wary of consuming too much sugar." _____

2. "Everyone knows we'll never get rid of poverty; that's just how it is." _____

3. "In places where handwashing is a frequent practice, cold and flu rates are much lower. We should be sure to wash our hands often." _____

4. "All electronics that come from China contain spyware." _____

Descriptions:

A) The assertion is based on a popular belief; it is a nonargument.

B) The assertion is based on arguments and conclusions provided by a reputable source.

C) The conclusion is unconfirmable. How could this possibly be corroborated?

D) This argument connects a premise and conclusion logically.

BEWARE OF PITFALLS

Examine the erroneous reasoning in each of the following statements, which are based on unfounded conclusions derived from certain false premises that appeal to authority, common beliefs, fear, or faulty generalizations. How would you respond to challenge these assertions?

1. "Many leading scientists dispute that climate change has occurred. It is therefore a hoax."

_____

_____

_____

2. "The representative of our district has been indicted for corruption. No surprise here; everyone knows all politicians are corrupt or untrustworthy."

_____

_____

_____

3. "Modern cars have airbags, so there's no need for me to wear a seat belt."

_____

_____

_____

4. "Yesterday I got cut off by a young driver. Young people are terrible drivers!"

_____

_____

_____

5. "My neighbor doesn't work; he depends on government assistance. What an opportunist!"

_____

_____

_____

This puzzle comes from none other than the great children's book writer and puzzle maker Lewis Carroll (1832–1898), author of *Alice's Adventures in Wonderland* and *Through the Looking-Glass, and What Alice Found There*.

You see two clocks on a table, both of which indicate that it is 12 o'clock. You are told that one doesn't work at all, while the other loses a minute of time every day. Which is the more accurate clock?

_____

_____

_____

Reconstructing Reasoning

Consider the following statement: "That phone costs more than the others. Therefore it must be better." The unspoken premise is that if something is more expensive, we should conclude that it's of higher quality. The problem is that this may sometimes be true, but not always. Reasoning involves putting premises together like a jigsaw puzzle. But sometimes we may be forcing the pieces to fit because they usually do, even if in this case they do not. Here are three examples:

1. If we find that something is healthy, like adding more nuts to our diet, we tend to generalize that this will be good for everyone. But this argument doesn't apply to someone who has a peanut allergy.

2. If we see that a new employee isn't wearing a wedding ring, we might assume she's not married. But not all married people wear rings.

3. If we find a certain brand of battery lasts longer in our smoke detectors, we might buy it again next time. But there may be even better batteries that we're not trying.

THE CONNECTION BETWEEN PREMISES AND CONCLUSIONS

The key to understanding how arguments work is to grasp how we tend to connect premises and conclusions. A premise suggests a conclusion. But even a premise that's factually correct can lead to false conclusions, if it's not connected in a logically sound way. For example, suppose we read that a series of church bombings is connected to a certain terrorist group. We then hear that another bombing has occurred. The premise (a terrorist group has bombed multiple churches) suggests a conclusion (they're also responsible for the latest attack). So our inclination is to blame that group. However, lacking concrete evidence to establish that connection, we cannot reach this conclusion. The latest bombing could be a copycat crime or completely unrelated to the others.

Premises and conclusions can be falsely connected in roundabout ways, leading to circular reasoning. Both sides of an argument say the same thing, so no true conclusion is reached. For example:

"These candies are delicious, since it says so on the package."

"You have to invite her, because it is important to invite her."

"The best place to live on earth is our nation, because it is better than any other nation."

Such reasoning has perplexed philosophers for millennia and has been the source of many famous paradoxes. The British puzzle maker Henry Dudeney (1857–1930) gave a concrete example in his book *Amusements in Mathematics*:

"A child asked, 'Can God do everything?' On receiving an affirmative reply, she at once said, 'Then can He make a stone so heavy that He can't lift it?'"

The child's question is a version of an ancient paradox: "What would happen if an irresistible moving body came into contact with an immovable body?" Well, Dudeney remarked, "if there existed such a thing as an immovable body, there could not at the same time exist a moving body that nothing could resist." And we all have heard the one about the chicken and the egg: "Which came first?" It was the chicken, of course. But then, a chicken comes from an egg. So, it was the egg. But then, an egg comes from a chicken. So, it was the chicken. And on and on in circles.

SPELLING OUT ASSUMPTIONS

To increase the chances that our arguments are logical and meaningful, we must always identify and spell out what assumptions they are based on or may be lurking behind them. Assumptions can be reasonable or not. It is the unreasonable ones that we must always attempt to identify. Common types of assumptions are the following:

Explicit assumption. An assumption stated overtly is an explicit assumption. It might be true or false, and is presented without proof. "China is trying to destroy our economy." "Funding space exploration will lead to technology breakthroughs."

Implicit assumption. In this case, an assumption is suggested or implied but not stated outright. "Our economic policy should penalize China." "We need to spend more on space exploration." An implicit assumption holds more potential danger, since it alludes to something by innuendo and may go unchallenged.

Factual assumption. This type of assumption includes a factual basis, one that can easily be verified. "The ASPCA says that Labrador retrievers are good pets for families with kids."

Analytical assumption. This type of assumption involves an interpretation or analysis of specific cases. "I've been around dogs my whole life, so I know that dogs are great companions."

Values-based assumption. This is an assumption that is based on moral or ethical concerns or values. By definition, it cannot be defended with reason; it can only be assumed to be correct if one agrees with the value system invoked. "Buying products from that company is immoral."

Bad reasoning as well as good reasoning is possible; and this fact is the foundation of the practical side of logic.

—**Charles Sanders Peirce**

IDENTIFY THE FAULTY REASONING

Here are examples of premises that lead to questionable conclusions. How would you analyze each of them to get at the truth?

1. "He is a great chef because he's incredible."

2. "Our team won yesterday because the coach kept changing players throughout the game. We're definitely going to make the playoffs and win the championship this year."

3. "I wouldn't take her advice about healthy eating; she's a vegetarian. They have strange ideas about nutrition."

4. "Why do you want to change our antiterrorist laws? You must not care about keeping people safe and protecting our national security."

_____

_____

_____

UNFOUNDED REASONING

Sometimes the fault in a faulty argument lies not in circular reasoning, a false premise, or unwarranted connections between a premise and a conclusion, but in a style of reasoning that is inherently flawed. Here are three common types of unfounded reasoning to watch out for.

Ad hominem reasoning. *Example:* "If you think this cartoon isn't funny, you're not smart enough to understand it." The tactic of *ad hominem* (Latin for "to the person") reasoning is meant to attack one's opponent, rather than what that person is saying. It shifts the argument away from the issue at hand—in this case, the humor of a particular cartoon—in an attempt to lure the other person into denying a personal accusation.

The excluded middle. *Example:* "We must first deal with crime in our society before dealing with pollution." In the fallacy of the excluded middle, a false either-or situation is invented. Why not attack both problems—crime and pollution—simultaneously, not in some exclusive, prioritized, or sequential way?

The straw man argument. *Example:* "You're not going to vote for her? So you don't think a woman can hold office?" This type of reasoning sets up a "straw man" to argue against. That is, it attacks a false representation of the opponent's argument, usually one that's easier to contest than what's really being presented.

Here is *the* classic puzzle in circular reasoning. It is called the Liar Paradox. If you have never come across it, let me warn you that it will make your head spin around in circles.

A certain poet named Epimenides was born and reared on the island of Crete. One day, he made the following statement: "All Cretans are liars!" Is his statement true or false? Explain your reasoning.

Bulletproof Logic

Arguments that connect premises in a way that makes a conclusion inescapable demonstrate how bulletproof logic works, even if, as we've seen, the conclusion is not necessarily true or the premises are false.

But what is logic? Is the logic that applies to proving theorems in mathematics the same logic that we use to solve everyday practical problems? The philosopher Charles Peirce differentiated between two kinds of logic—*logica utens* (a useful or practical logic) and *logica docens* (a theoretical or learned logic). The former is a rudimentary form of reasoning that we all possess without being able to specify what it is. The latter is a sophisticated and tutored use of logic practiced by, well, logicians and critical thinkers!

In a sense, we spend our entire day solving problems in practical logic without knowing it. For example, let's say you can't find your car keys in the morning after eating breakfast. If you look around randomly for them, you might be lucky and find them. But if this doesn't work out, logic kicks in: "Did I have the keys with me this morning before breakfast?" If the answer is yes, then a subsequent logical question would be: "Where could I have put them mindlessly?" That question might lead you to retrace your steps and, in all likelihood, lead you to locating your lost keys.

Here is a paraphrase of a classic puzzle in logical reasoning. It was invented in the 1930s by the British puzzlist Hubert Phillips, who was known among his readers as "Caliban," after the grotesque character in Shakespeare's *The Tempest*.

In a society hidden away on an island in the Pacific, there are two types of citizens—the Truthers and the Liars. The former always tell the truth, no matter what; the latter always, absolutely always, lie. We visit the island and come across three male citizens. "Are you a Truther or a Liar?" we ask one of them. "Juju," replies the man. "What did he say?" we ask the second and third individuals. "He said that he is a Truther," said the second one in plain English. "No, he said that he was a Liar," countered the third. Can you figure out what type (Truther or Liar) the second and third individuals are?

DEDUCTIVE REASONING

Bulletproof logic is based on deriving a singular and inescapable conclusion from certain premises, without reference to external information. This type of reasoning is called *deductive*. Its structure is shown in formal terms by the syllogism. Let's revisit the concept of syllogism here for the sake of convenience:

Major premise: All dogs have a powerful sense of smell.

Minor premise: Lucy is a dog.

Conclusion: Lucy has a powerful sense of smell.

The conclusion is iron-clad, even though it may not be necessarily true in reality. Poor Lucy may have lost her sense of smell through some unfortunate accident—a real-life possibility that can never be eliminated. But this is external information; it does not impugn the logic used. The validity (or invalidity) of an argument depends on its structure, not on the truth or falsity of its premises. In other words: A sound argument is not necessarily true.

Now, while the above syllogism was laid out formally, with its premises and conclusion labeled, in real life it tends to be an unconscious structure, implicit in everyday speech. Here are some examples:

Wool makes me itch (major premise); this blanket makes me itch (minor premise); the blanket must be made of wool (conclusion).

My boyfriend cooks terrible pancakes (major premise); he just made some pancakes for breakfast (minor premise); they're going to taste awful (conclusion).

Santa Claus comes every Christmas Eve and leaves gifts down the chimney (major premise); there are gifts under the tree on Christmas morning (minor premise); they were left by Santa (conclusion).

If any of those premises are false—and we're not saying any are—our conclusion may not be true, even though it logically follows. How can we be certain that a sound argument is also true?

DEDUCTIVE PROOF

The answer is to bolster our deductive reasoning with proof. So for the three prior deductions, deductive truth might be achieved as follows:

Itchy blanket: Checking the product label will reveal that our conclusion is correct. Or it may reveal that there's another fabric we're allergic to.

Pancakes: The proof is in the pudding, or in the tasting. But if we want to spare ourselves the experience, we could ask whether the cook has tried a different recipe this time, casting our conclusion into doubt.

Santa Claus: We might try staying up late to see if we can catch him in the act. Or failing that, ask a trustworthy witness like a parent to try and snap a picture. Though really, Santa's existence is so well documented, why question it?

VALID REASONING

Valid reasoning is another way of saying "correct deductive reasoning." An argument is valid if the premises lead to an inescapable conclusion. To put it another way, if the premises of the argument are true, then the conclusion cannot be false. If it is true that everyone dies, then it is an inescapable conclusion that we, too, will one day die. It's that simple.

Reasoning does not necessarily have to apply to the real world; a valid argument can also occur in the imagination. For example, suppose in a sci-fi movie, robots have taken over the world but without exception have a built-in mechanism that limits their life. Then, as in the case of real-world human mortality, in this fiction it's an inescapable conclusion that the "hero robot" of the story will also eventually die.

INVALID REASONING

Invalid reasoning means deriving conclusions that do not conform to the premises of an argument. In the examples above, it would be invalid reasoning to conclude that a human, or a robot, will never die.

Often common sense will tell us that a line of reasoning is invalid. But not always. One does not need to use formal logic to accept this as true. However, common sense does not always reveal the validity of the logic in not-so-obvious arguments. Here is an example.

No frongs are glerbish.

Children are not glerbish.

Therefore children are frongs.

What can we make of this? Since we don't know the meaning of the made-up words "frong" or "glerbish," common sense isn't helpful. But the conclusion makes no sense logically. The confusing element is the use of the two negatives—there's nothing in the premise that says that everything that isn't glerbish is also a frong. So by the premises of this argument, it's possible for a child to not be a frong. Here's a tip: A rule of deductive logic is that no valid argument has two negative premises, so be suspicious anytime you spot that in an argument.

———————————

If it was so, it might be; and if it were so, it would be; but as it isn't, it ain't. That's logic.

—Lewis Carroll

VALID OR INVALID?

Let's try out some straightforward reasoning. For each example, decide whether the argument is valid—even if not realistic.

1. "All elephants can fly. Dumbo is an elephant. Therefore he can fly."

2. "All actors are robots. Brad Pitt is an actor. So he, too, is a robot."

3. "No robots are sensitive. Some dogs are not sensitive. Therefore some dogs are robots."

BEWARE OF FAULTY DEDUCTIONS!

What are the expected deductions that the following statements assume? Indicate what kind of deductive proof is warranted.

1. "University degrees lead to good jobs. I got my degree last month."

2. "A poll showed that social media users developed a form of amnesia, whereby they could not remember what they said on social media the day before. Jerry is on social media every day."

_____

_____

_____

3. "Since Mr. Tindell was elected mayor, there are more people unemployed than ever before."

_____

_____

_____

This deductive reasoning puzzle again comes from the mind of Henry Dudeney, whom we encountered earlier. He was a master maker of logic puzzles. Here is a paraphrase of one of his classic puzzles.

In a high-tech company, Amy, Sharma, and Sarah hold the positions of programmer, analyst, and software engineer, but not necessarily in that order. The software engineer is an only child. She also earns the least of the three. Sarah married Amy's brother a few years ago. She earns more than the analyst. What position does each person fill?

Probable and Possible

The previous section dealt with bulletproof logic. But life is not always so logical. Many times, we must draw probable or possible conclusions. In this case, rather than *deduction*, the logic is called *induction*. Inductive reasoning is based on the idea that if something occurs often, we must conclude that there is likely some reason behind it.

Probability is the likelihood that something will happen, given previous experience or knowledge. Dark clouds are typical signs of rain, but rain may not necessarily ensue. The rain is *probable*, not *certain*. Possibility is something that is conceivable, but not necessarily likely. "Is it possible to live longer by eating well?" The answer is yes, but because there are other factors that affect life span, we can't say that healthy eating will have an influence greater than something else.

Thinking in terms of likely possibilities can lead us astray. We might label anything that fits in with our particular worldview or prejudices as possible or probable.

Inductive reasoning helps us be more accurate in cases such as those just mentioned. It involves extrapolation—extracting from a set of observations, facts, and premises a conclusion that is highly probable but not certain. It exemplifies what we commonly describe as "making an informed guess."

PROBABILITY/RATIONAL EXPECTATION

Reasoning by induction is drawing a likely general conclusion from a pattern seen in particular cases. If numerous cases under consideration point to a specific pattern or result, then the probability that the result is accurate is high. This type of reasoning is used all the time in science. For example, if a certain drug is found to eliminate a certain virus in a large number of patients, then we can draw the inference that it's probably effective for most people. But in order to assert this, the drug must be tested with subsequent patients to check the consistency of the results. The more the same pattern of results is found, the more confidence we can have.

CASE STUDY: *EINSTEIN AND ANALOGY*

Analogy-making shows the way that many scientists think. Analogies, like inductions, are based on observing things in the world and establishing a linkage among them. They are also used to make something understandable.

Einstein's theory of relativity is often explained with the following type of analogy. Imagine that we are on a smoothly running train, which is moving at a constant velocity. Inside the train we may drop a book, or throw a ball to someone else back and forth. The book will appear to fall straight down when it is dropped; the ball will appear to travel directly from the thrower to the catcher. All these actions can be carried on in the same way and with the same results on the ground outside the moving train. As long as the train runs smoothly, with constant velocity, none of these activities will be affected by its motion. But if the train stops or speeds up abruptly, the structure of the activities will change. A book may be jarred from a seat and fall without being dropped. A ball will move differently back and forth. In effect, the laws of motion will remain the same on the ground and in a train if the train is moving smoothly. In more technical language: If two systems move uniformly relative to each other, then the laws of physics are the same in both systems.

PROBABLE OR POSSIBLE?

Indicate the type of reasoning involved in the following as either deductive or inductive.

1. **Insomnia cure?** A certain drug was tested on 100 subjects suffering from insomnia, and it was found that in 94 percent of the subjects sleeping patterns improved considerably.

2. **Helping those in need.** Grant money has been given to your department for a project to assess food insecurity in under-privileged neighborhoods. Since you manage the project, you know that you will need a bigger budget to work with.

3. **Side effect.** Studies show a medication for pain relief often causes anxiety if overused. You conclude that if you take too much of it, you, too, might start feeling anxious and nervous.

We live in a fantasy world, a world of illusion.
The great task in life is to find reality.

—Iris Murdoch

INDUCTION PITFALLS

Like deduction, inductive reasoning may involve ambiguity or misrepresentation. The reasoning may be logically sound, but the truthfulness of the conclusion in the real world depends on the credibility of the evidence it's based on. What is the expected induction for each case? What factors might affect your confidence in that conclusion?

1. "Every time I see Debbie eat peanuts, she starts sneezing."

_____

_____

_____

2. "My dad smoked a packet of cigarettes per day and never got lung cancer. So, too, did my uncle and other family members. I also smoke a pack a day."

_____

_____

_____

3. "A survey revealed that 3 out of 4 dentists recommend toothpaste brand X."

_____

_____

_____

The Essentials of Explanations, Theories, and Hypotheses

The art of reasoning is also the art of explaining. If the reasoning is sound, it can convince us to accept an explanation, even if it is contrary to what we expect—a key feature of critical thinking. This is how new scientific theories become established, sometimes upending our existing understanding of how the world works. If the theory masquerades as being sound but is not—if it's pseudoscientific—we can be led into believing something that's not true simply because it has the sheen of a well-reasoned argument. It's important to remember that explanations and theories are only accurate if the information on which they are based is accurate. In other words, garbage in, garbage out.

Keep all that in mind, and you should be relatively immune to these common pseudoscientific forms of reasoning:

Explanations presented as fact. Explanations are statements that make something clear or understandable: "Population trends depend on the birth rate." But explanations can also be used to justify an action or belief: "They rejected my application because they are biased against younger people." An explanation without proof to back it up isn't necessarily true, even if it sounds believable.

Theories promoted as truth. Theories are explanations that are developed to apply broadly to similar phenomena: "The theory of evolution is based on evidence that different complex organisms have developed from earlier and simpler forms." Some theories are true because of evidence, not just because they're phrased authoritatively. Some theories are wrong. Someone might state, "The theory that the earth is flat is proven by the evidence of our eyes, since we walk on a flat terrain, not a round one." But we know that better evidence proves the theory to be wrong.

Untested hypotheses. A hypothesis is a tentative explanation made on the basis of limited evidence, which must be tested further to ensure its validity. People are always coming up with unlikely hypotheses and presenting them without evidence as if they've been confirmed. "If we legalize marijuana, then we will end up legalizing all drugs" is an untested hypothesis—looking at examples in other countries shows no evidence that this is true.

FALSE LOGIC RED FLAGS

We must always be wary of the mechanisms of false logic. Here are some red flags that should always prompt you to take a closer look at an assertion to see whether a seemingly logical statement stands up to scrutiny.

If A, then B. This kind of reasoning seems to causally connect things. But a cause-and-effect connection is not always the case.

Thus/Therefore. We are accustomed to using these adverbs to signal a conclusion. Arguments that employ them should always be viewed with caution, because the presence of a conclusion doesn't always mean the logic was valid.

Since. This is used typically to support some premise, whether founded or not. Be wary of clauses introduced with this conjunction, which might cause you to gloss over a flawed argument.

Because. This conjunction is used typically to rationalize an explanation or conclusion; make sure it's an earned conclusion.

THE SCIENTIFIC METHOD

The scientific method does not rely on logic alone—it requires proof and significance-testing as well. (The latter has a special designation in science; without going into the mathematical details, suffice it to say that results are tested to be sure they're not a statistical fluke.)

For example, an initial hypothesis might be "Getting better grades correlates with getting better sleep." An appropriate sample of students with good grades is chosen, along with a comparable group of students with poorer grades. They are asked about their sleeping habits. The results are compiled and correlated to grades. If there is a correlation, then the hypothesis is proved. If not, then the hypothesis is discarded. In either case, further hypothesis testing might be useful.

Truth is stranger than fiction but it is because fiction is obliged to stick to possibilities; truth isn't.

—**Mark Twain**

PSEUDOSCIENCE

What are the red flags that suggest these statements need a second look?

Statement: "I keep a quartz crystal on my desk, since its energy helps me concentrate and improves my memory."

Statement: "Oxygen is bad for germs and bacteria; therefore covering a wound will delay healing."

_____

_____

Statement: "If my knees and elbows start to ache, then it's bound to rain in the next few days."

_____

_____

_____

THEORY TESTING

Here are some research results that you might find published in scientific journals. What's the most plausible theory to draw from each study? Match each study with a theory from the list below.

1. A large sample of children were given riddles and jigsaw puzzles to solve during recess at school. A similar group was not. Over time, the children who did the riddles and puzzles showed a greater achievement in virtually all subjects compared to the other group.

_____

_____

2. A group of older adults were taught a foreign language. After two years of learning, they were tested on memory skills. The results

showed that they had a higher level of memory retention when compared to those who did not learn a language.

_____

_____

_____

3. A large group of children diagnosed with attention deficit disorder (ADD) were administered a set of reading tasks as part of their education over two years, with the consent and help of their parents or caretakers. The results showed a significant improvement in attention spans when compared to a matched group that was not administered the tasks.

_____

_____

_____

Possible theories:

A) Kids with ADD need extra help learning to read.

B) Kids who do puzzles pay more attention in class.

C) Learning another language later in life might help combat memory problems.

D) Problem-solving enhances learning.

E) Memory improves with age.

F) Reading enhances attention.

The "Drawing Out Puzzle," invented by Martin Gardner, is a logic puzzle that demonstrates hypothesis testing.

In a box there are 10 balls, 5 white and 5 black. What is the least number of balls you must draw from the box in order to guarantee a pair that matches in color (two white or two black)? Explain your reasoning.

_____

_____

_____

_____

Key Takeaways: CHAPTER 2

*When dealing with people, remember
you are not dealing with creatures of logic,
but creatures of emotion.*

—Dale Carnegie

Let's sum up the main points to take away from this chapter.

1. Beware of the many pitfalls that the unconscious structure of logical reasoning can produce.

2. Be especially wary of circular arguments.

3. Always ask for evidence for a theory or explanation.

4. Always be open to changing your mind on the basis of new information or evidence.

5. Our minds are constantly searching for and devising explanations to account for common experiences and new information. In science, this propensity leads to theories that are then tested for validation. However, the same tendency is behind pseudoscientific theories.

6. Beware of the misuse of logic based on beliefs or false reasoning. If a premise of an argument isn't true, the conclusions may not be true, even if the logic is sound.

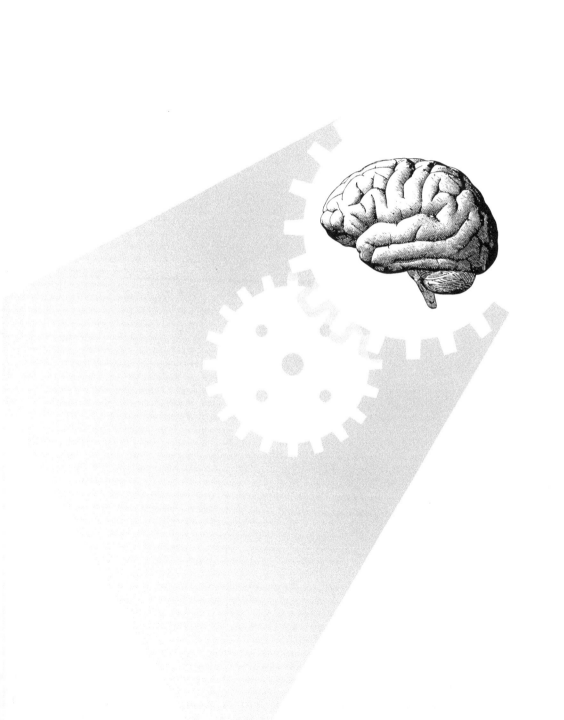

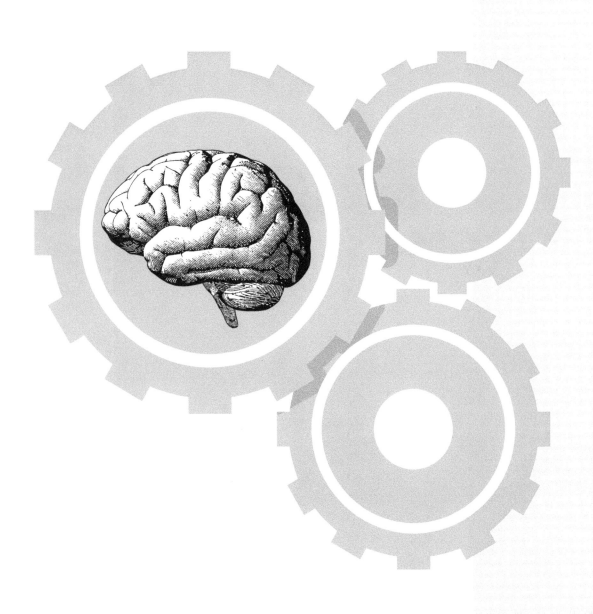

CHAPTER 3

Rhetoric, Fallacy, and Bias

One of the most lovable comic strips of all time is *Peanuts,* by Charles Schulz. Its characters are metaphors of real-life personalities. One of them is the famously crabby Lucy, who dispenses advice and opinions with great facility. She certainly knows how to manipulate Charlie Brown with her arguments. And he always falls for them. Lucy exemplifies how language can be used to persuade others, even if the argument is invalid.

Here's one of my favorite exchanges between Lucy and Charlie Brown (Charles Schulz, *The Peanuts Treasury*, 1968):

Charlie Brown: Next year I'm going to be a changed person.

Lucy: That's a laugh, Charlie Brown.

Charlie Brown: I mean it! I'm going to be strong and firm!

Lucy: Forget it. You'll always be wishy-washy!

Charlie Brown: Why can't I change just a little bit? (*Shouts*) I'll be wishy one day and washy the next!

See how expertly Lucy undermined poor Charlie Brown's confidence? He became so focused on her use of the word "wishy-washy" that he abandoned his claim and practically admitted she was right.

In the previous chapter we looked at how arguments unfold through logical processes. As Charlie Brown kept finding out, these can be manipulated by language. So it's time to look more closely at the connection between arguments and language. This chapter will cover these main topics:

- What rhetoric is and what it allows you to do

- The main logical fallacies and how they're framed linguistically

- The two main types of biases (cognitive and behavioral) that you should always be on the alert for

Rhetoric: The Lay of the Land

Language is a unique human trait. We use it not only to communicate information and to express ourselves in specific ways, but also to think about things, to bring about changes in our lives, and to persuade people to do something that they may otherwise not do.

Persuasive language falls under the rubric of *rhetoric*, defined as the study of how language is designed to be effective communicatively and emotionally. Recognizing the devices that make an argument rhetorically impactful is an important skill for critical thinking, since persuasion is an essential part of how we communicate, for good or ill. President John F. Kennedy's inaugural speech, in which he exhorted the public to "ask not what your country can do for you, ask what you can do for your country," and Martin Luther King's "I Have a Dream" speech are masterful examples of how great orators use rhetorical speech to make their points effective. Of course, dictators also make speeches, which have persuaded people to follow them even to their own detriment. Clearly, understanding rhetorical devices will help us draw smart conclusions.

For example, when someone says, "You won't regret it," implying "You will be happy with it," that person is using the rhetorical strategy called *litotes*, which allows the person to emphasize something indirectly in an effort to block any effective logical retort. Metaphorical statements are also highly persuasive, because they play on images in our minds that are hard to eradicate: "Stay away from him; he's a snake."

There are many such devices, but the following eight are among the most common.

Rhetorical questions. Perhaps illustrating the most familiar use of the term "rhetoric," these are statements phrased in the form of questions but not intended to be answered. Rather, a rhetorical question is used to assert something, gain consensus, produce a dramatic effect, or attain some other deliberate end. Rhetorical questions are typically framed in such a way as to inhibit a listener from disagreeing and are often phrased in a negative way: "Is there nothing sacred anymore in our society?" They can also be used to reinforce something already asserted: "How can you argue against this?" They might be used for satirical effect, emphasizing that something is blatantly obvious: "He lost his job again. Duh, who would have thought?" Whatever the variation, rhetorical questions are designed to block true dialogue and skew an argument in favor of the speaker. Can you believe people do this?

Jargon. Jargon comes in two forms—one useful and one potentially dangerous. The former is the kind of specialized language used by professionals or organizations to make communication among members concrete, specific, and efficient. For instance, doctors might use the following words to be precise medically: *hematoma* for blood clot, *pruritis* for itchiness, and *pustule* for a pimple with pus. The second type of jargon exemplifies speech designed to be diplomatic or polite, blunting the impact of more direct wording: "There is a negative cash flow at this time" (We're broke); "We've decided to reorganize" (You're fired); and so on.

Buzzwords. "Think outside the box." "Our company is a disruptor." "We need some evergreen marketing." Buzzwords are terms and phrases that are in vogue and typically used without reflection, communicating very little substantive content in an attempt to seem in the forefront of politics, advertising, pop culture, or some profession or business. They can catch on and gain wide use outside their original context. The danger is that they deflect us away from what is really being said or create the appearance of expertise when there's nothing behind them. Buzzwords are similar to jargon. But jargon tends to be specialized vocabulary used by specific groups of people; buzzwords are expressions that catch on broadly. The two may overlap, of course. Online marketers are quite adept at using buzzwords to turbocharge engagement, harvest higher response rates, and generate click-through.

Euphemisms. These are milder or more polite words or phrases used in place of something embarrassing, offensive, or dreadful. Familiar examples include *passed away* for died, *let go* for fired, and *hooking up* for having sex. Euphemisms typically refer to taboo subjects such as sex, defecation, and death in a more gracious or genteel way—*the birds and the bees* for sex, *bowel movement* for defecation, *marital aids* for sex toys, *departed* for died. But they can also hide biases or prejudices or deceitfully soften the truth—*collateral damage* for killing civilians. Like jargon and buzzwords, euphemisms can (and often do) fall into the category of doublespeak—language that misrepresents or conceals to deceive. As you can see, a euphemism might be a genuine attempt at politeness, but it could also be pure baloney.

Hyperbole. "That suitcase weighed a ton." "I've been doing this forever." "She has been my friend since the beginning of time." This type of exaggeration is known as hyperbole, or the technique of overstating something to highlight it or to create the belief that it is more important or bigger than it actually is. One of the best-known historical examples of the latter is P. T. Barnum's description of his circus as "The greatest show on earth!" Hyperbole is effective in advertising, politics, and other social spheres. We must always be wary of it! If we abuse hyperbole, we risk permanently destroying our credibility beyond all repair.

Ellipsis. Sometimes not saying something overtly is more effective: "You know that this is something that you and I have always . . . No need to fill in the blanks, right?" Intentional omission of a word or phrase or allusion to something unspoken both calls attention to it and invites the listener to fill in the blanks. Incomplete expressions such as "I never thought . . ." or "They say . . ." are typical examples of this strategy. By the way, you can always recognize ellipsis in print by looking for those three dots . . .

Climax. This is the strategy of arranging the parts of an argument in an increasing order of their importance, from the least to the most important. We react emotionally to this crescendo, seeing it as an argument's point of arrival: "He first seemed to make a simple blunder, but it soon became obvious that it was a clever form of deceit and maybe even treachery." Climax is often used in advertising to create a false comparison: "Product A is good; B is better; but ours is best!" Anytime we put three concepts in a row in such a way, rhetorical climax is created: the third in the list automatically seems to be the most important. Take faith, hope, and love. Arrange these in different ways, and you will see what I mean. Here's one way: "We must always have hope, which comes from love, and should lead us to faith." This strategy is particularly effective because it can catch your attention, keep you hooked, and completely transform your opinion of almost anything.

Anticlimax. This is the opposite strategy of climax and arranges the parts of an argument in decreasing order of importance. It incorporates a surprise factor that catches the listener's attention. This technique is often used for ironic or satirical effect: "I will knock down his ideas first, and then I will listen to him." This may be the most devastating type of rhetoric, except for all the others.

These rhetorical devices are used not only by persuasive speakers but by everyone as part of their everyday discourse, even though we hardly ever realize we're doing it. Since we have all absorbed this kind of language from childhood onward, we are susceptible to it at an unconscious level. This is why it is essential to recognize it.

Rhetoric may be defined as the faculty of observing in any given case the available means of persuasion. This is not a function of any other art.

—Aristotle

CASE STUDY: *A CLASSIC RHETORICAL QUESTION*

One of the more famous lines from Shakespeare is in *Julius Caesar*, act 3, scene 1: *"Et tu, Brute?"* The line—Latin for "You too, Brutus?"—is spoken by Julius Caesar to his presumed friend and protégé Marcus Brutus, who's among the assassins stabbing Caesar. There's no historical record of Caesar uttering anything before his death; the line was created by Shakespeare to great effect, eliciting pathos for Caesar's plight. In his inimitable way, Shakespeare brings the event into the sphere of everybody's understanding, making us feel for Caesar as someone who was betrayed by a close ally.

The one-liner packs more meaning than if Caesar had made a verbose speech about the emotional destruction caused by a friend's unexpected betrayal. It's a classic example of a rhetorical question, making the sense of betrayal highly dramatic, allowing Caesar to convey his emotions tersely and pathetically. It is truly fascinating to observe how one single rhetorical question can contain so much meaning.

There is an obvious cautionary subtext to this story: beware of even your closest friends, since they may betray you at any moment. The actual episode in Roman history is a poignant reminder that self-serving passions and personal calculations always play a role in altering the course of human life. As provided by Shakespeare, Caesar's question is a one-sentence cautionary political tale that continues to have resonance to this day.

IDENTIFY THE STRATEGY

Becoming aware of how rhetoric pervades speech is a key critical-thinking skill. This exercise is intended to help you hone your recognition skills. Identify the strategy used in each statement—rhetorical question, jargon, buzzword, euphemism, hyperbole, ellipsis, climax, or anticlimax. To make this exercise a little more interesting, the statements are taken from literary or historically significant sources.

1. "What made you think of love and tears and birth and death and pain?"

2. "This note was a promise that all men, yes, black men as well as white men, would be guaranteed the 'unalienable Rights' of 'Life, Liberty and the pursuit of Happiness.'"

3. "'The Answer to the Great Question . . . of Life, the Universe and Everything . . . [is] . . . Forty-two,' said Deep Thought, with infinite majesty and calm."

4. "The Ministry of Truth, which concerned itself with news, entertainment, education, and the fine arts; the Ministry of Peace, which concerned itself with war; the Ministry of Love, which maintained law and order; and the Ministry of Plenty, which was responsible for economic affairs. Their names, in Newspeak: Minitrue, Minipax, Miniluv, and Miniplenty."

5. "So, he's proactive, huh?" "Oh, God, yes. We're talking about a totally outrageous paradigm."

6. "My aunt fingered the stem of her wine-glass before sipping a little. 'Did he . . . peacefully?' she asked."

7. "Son of a Bludger."

8. "Will all great Neptune's ocean wash this blood clean from my hand?"

WHAT'S INTENDED?

Below is a list of buzzword- and jargon-rich phrases. Can you identify the meaning of each? Match the statement with the intention. For extra credit, guess if the term is a buzzword or jargon.

1. "It's fat-free; it must be healthy."

2. "Look at the bigger picture."

3. "We are now undergoing a paradigm shift."

_____

4. "Did you take all parameters into account?"

_____

5. "We must go forward and move the needle drastically."

_____

6. "After all is said and done, that's the bottom line."

_____

7. "Well, at the end of the day, all this amounts to nothing."

_____

Meanings:

A) Change a situation in a noticeable way

B) Ultimate outcome

C) When everything is taken into account

D) Characteristic numerical pattern in a sample or population

E) Not containing fats, animal or vegetable

F) Fundamental change in existing ideas or underlying premises

G) Understanding a situation beyond the present

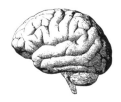

TYPES OF IRONY

Verbal. This is the most common type and uses words to mean the opposite in order to emphasize something or make an unexpected comparison: "It is really nice outside" (uttered during a hurricane).

Situational. This type of irony is used to signal the difference between what is expected (or what *should be*) and what happens (or *actually is*). An example would be the irony of flying in a plane where the pilot is afraid of flying.

Dramatic. This is used often in drama; it occurs when the audience is aware of something that the character on stage is not aware of. The most famous example is in the play *Oedipus Rex* (c. 429 BCE) by Sophocles, in which the audience knows that the person whom Oedipus killed, Laius, was his father, as Oedipus tries to figure it out.

Seeing Through Fallacies

We have come across examples of fallacious reasoning in previous chapters. Now let's focus on the language behind fallacies, so as to make it easier to detect a faulty or deliberately deceptive argument.

Fallacies can be divided into three main categories, which go back to ancient rhetorical analysis.

Pathos. This describes fallacies that are designed to appeal to the emotions. For example, "Displaying the flag means being patriotic." We cannot assume that anyone who hangs a flag is genuinely patriotic—the person could be doing it for some clever self-serving reason.

Ethos. This describes fallacies that are intended to appeal to our sense of ethics. For example, "That bank manager is responsible for the collapse of the bank." Since the manager stands for the bank, it is easy to blame the manager for its failure, while the truth may be something quite different. We must always be wary of arguments that appeal to our ethical sense.

Logos. This describes arguments that lead to fallacious conclusions. The term is a more technical and precise way of saying that a conclusion does not follow logically from the premises (as we discussed in the previous chapter). For example, "Conservative policies are generally for the well-off; that politician does not support the underprivileged, so he must be a conservative." Apart from the fact that the major premise about conservatives may be a false assumption, it certainly cannot be concluded that the politician in question is a conservative. There could be other categories of political belief that don't support underprivileged people.

SEE IT AND DON'T BELIEVE IT

For critical thinkers, the expression *seeing is believing* could be adapted as *see it and don't believe it*, to indicate that we should always try to spot arguments based on pathos, ethos, and logos. Consider the following statements:

"You should buy domestic to keep our economy strong." This is a pathos appeal to patriotism that doesn't offer any support for the claim it makes.

"So you believe crime victims don't have any rights?" This ethos-based argument uses a rhetorical question to challenge someone's sense of justice.

"If you vote for that politician, our society will collapse." This is a logos fallacy, with a conclusion that doesn't follow logically from the premise.

THE DECEPTIVE DOZEN

Logical fallacies aren't always easy to spot. To help you stay on the lookout, here's a roundup of the 12 most common types and advice on how to handle them.

1. **Straw man fallacy.** As mentioned in the last chapter, this is an argument in which someone refutes a distorted version of their opponent's position, not what they actually said.

   Example: "Adolescents should be taught about safe sex in school." "So, you think kids should have sex?"

   How to respond: Pressure your opponent to reveal their straw man. "Why do you think I'm saying kids should have sex?"

2. **Bandwagon fallacy.** This refers to any argument that concludes that if many people believe something, then it must be true.

   Example: "Everyone uses an iPhone; you should, too."

   How to respond: "Just because everyone says it's a great phone, that doesn't make it true. Give me facts."

3. **Appeal to authority fallacy.** This argument claims that something is true or false because an expert or some authoritative figure or celebrity says it is so.

   Example: "There are plenty of studies showing that eating chocolate is good for you."

   How to respond: "I'll accept evidence from sources that can be identified as reputable and legitimate, not hearsay."

4. **False dilemma fallacy.** This is the presentation of two opposing options—the dilemma—with the intention of concealing or eliminating other alternatives.

   > ***Example:*** "We must cut the welfare budget, because we cannot go deeper into debt."

   > ***How to respond:*** Point out that there are more possibilities involved. "We can avoid debt by other means and keep the welfare budget as it is."

5. **Hasty generalization fallacy.** This argument generalizes something on scarce, sketchy, or faulty evidence, like a single example or anecdote.

   > ***Example:*** "They fired that young guy the other day for not finishing any of his projects. Millennials are just lazy."

   > ***How to respond:*** Offer a counterexample. "Lori in accounting is in her 20s, and she's been promoted three times in the last year."

6. **Slothful induction fallacy.** This is the opposite of the previous fallacy. Instead of drawing an unwarranted connection, it's used to deny an assertion that's supported by facts, dismissing it as mere coincidence.

   > ***Example:*** "The oceans aren't getting warmer because of climate change; they've always warmed up from time to time; we just happen to be in that period now."

   > ***How to respond:*** "Is there any evidence that can confirm what you're saying, since I've provided facts to the contrary?"

7. **Correlation/causation fallacy.** This involves correlating two things causally—assuming one caused the other—just because they occur together or have a superficial connection.

   > ***Example:*** "Marriage rates increase with celibacy rates."

How to respond: Get the interlocutor to explain how their proposed connection between marriage and celibacy works. Ask "How so?"

8. **Anecdotal evidence fallacy.** This type of reasoning relies on personal observations or testimony, rather than evidence that's been collected scientifically.

   Example: "My brother's been vaping for years and hasn't had any health problems, so I know it's safe."

   How to respond: Offer a counterexample. "What about the people in this news story I found in a major, reputable newspaper, whose health took a nosedive after they started vaping?"

9. **Texas sharpshooter fallacy.** This term supposedly derives from the case of a certain Texan who shot bullets at the side of his barn, painted a target around the smallest cluster of bullet holes, and from this declared himself to be a sharpshooter. It refers to choosing data selectively and ignoring anything that does not support a conclusion.

   Example: "If you're a Pisces, you must be artistic. I know three artists who are Pisces."

   How to respond: "What about all the artists who weren't born under Pisces?" Or "So, what about people with that sign who aren't artistic at all? You're ignoring examples that don't agree with what you believe."

10. **Middle ground fallacy.** This type of argument assumes that when opposing arguments have purported merit, then the real answer must lie somewhere in the middle ground between them.

    Example: "Researchers say that vaccines don't cause serious illness, but lots of people believe they do. Probably some vaccines cause problems, others don't."

    How to respond: "So you believe both sides? Even though one side has so much more evidence?"

11. **Burden of proof fallacy.** This strategy shifts the burden of proof to the other person, evading the need to support one's claims.

> **Example:** "If you're so sure that there's no such thing as ghosts, prove they don't exist."

> **How to respond:** Demand equal terms. "Here's some evidence for my argument (provide examples of famous hoaxes). Where's your evidence?"

12. **Personal incredulity fallacy.** This involves assuming that if something seems incredible or implausible, then it must be wrong. It often appeals to false common sense.

> **Example:** "Obviously the sun moves around the earth, Galileo! Just look in the sky, how could it be otherwise?"

> **How to respond:** Galileo might have answered as follows: "Plenty of things seem unbelievable until they're proven. Have I shown you my telescope?"

Fallacies do not cease to be fallacies because they become fashions.

—G. K. Chesterton

CASE STUDY: *"I HAVE A DREAM!"* THE RHETORICAL POWER OF MARTIN LUTHER KING'S CLASSIC SPEECH

One of the greatest fighters for social justice and seekers of truth was the late Martin Luther King, Jr. (1929–1968). His speeches are classic examples of how rhetoric can be used for good. One of his most significant addresses is the "I Have a Dream" speech, which he delivered in Washington, DC, on August 28, 1963, during the March on Washington for Jobs and Freedom.

Here's an excerpt:

"Let us not wallow in the valley of despair. I say to you today, my friends, though, even though we face the difficulties of today and tomorrow, I still have a dream. It is a dream deeply rooted in the American dream."

The speech connects the plight of the Black community to the American Dream, which had never been a possibility for many. Using religious imagery effectively—"wallowing in the valley of despair"—King implores his fellow citizens to transcend that valley and dream the American Dream from a new vantage point. The implication is that those who dream bring forth the future.

IDENTIFY THE
DECEPTIVE DOZEN

In this exercise, identify what fallacy is involved in each statement.

1. "Those who rant against that politician are not true Americans. To put it another way—either you are for him, or you are anti-American."

2. "Everyone is buying that app; it is on sale. You can't let this opportunity go."

3. "Our pastor says that watching that sitcom will lead to immorality."

4. "Just because I was in 10 accidents last month after drinking a glass or two of wine doesn't mean that drinking and driving accidents are linked in any way."

5. "Crime rates increase as rates of watching violent TV increase."

6. "That criminal was released yesterday, and he committed another crime. Clearly, criminals do not get the punishment they deserve."

7. "My friend read online that drinking tea causes insomnia. I read instead that it calms the nerves, allowing us to sleep better. What do you think?" "I think that it is probably a bit of both."

8. "I cannot imagine how this could be true. How can scientists truly clone organisms? It goes against the odds. It is definitely impossible."

9. "The different phases of the moon, not global warming, are responsible for the rise in average temperature. Show me that I am wrong."

10. "The collapse of that bank was inevitable—look at all the accounts that show deficits."

11. "Last night a group of teenagers vandalized that store. Teenagers are so irresponsible."

12. "The city government should not build special bike lanes. Cyclists are always going through red lights and breaking all kinds of laws."

IDENTIFY THE STRATEGY

Determine what rhetorical strategy each of the following arguments displays—pathos, ethos, or logos.

The argument: Poor people siphon off a lot of resources from the economy, unfairly harming everyone, and so should not receive benefits or special treatment. Everyone should be treated equally; the poor should not be given special benefits by the government.

The argument: Marriage is a union between a man and a woman, as tradition dictates. It has always been that way, throughout history, and it's the way we've all been raised.

The argument: The rise in crime rates and violence by young people is due to the aggressive lyrics and music they listen to.

Cognitive and Behavioral Bias

The greatest danger connected with fallacious rhetorical arguments is that they can penetrate the mind and alter it—shaping beliefs and generating biases. Once a pattern of thinking becomes habit, it can be almost impossible to eradicate. Two types of biases can arise.

COGNITIVE BIAS

An error in reasoning that systematically affects how we think is termed a *cognitive bias*. For example, consider the belief that artistic creativity and left-handedness are interconnected. If we accept this as true, every time we come across a left-handed person who also happens to be artistic, we use it to confirm that belief. We might ignore incidences of the opposite case—say, a left-hander who is a mathematician. This is also known as *confirmation bias*. It privileges a particular idea by selectively ignoring contrary evidence.

Example: Holocaust denial is a bias based on a false belief—namely that the Holocaust did not take place or, at the very least, was not as bad as is claimed, despite overwhelming evidence to the contrary.

BEHAVIORAL BIAS

Behavioral bias results when a belief causes us to make decisions or take actions based on that belief. For example, we could hold a behavioral bias against a certain group and decide not to have anything to do with them, even if this is counterproductive.

Example: An employer needs to hire for a specific job but has difficulty finding someone. An immigrant applies for the job, but he is immediately eliminated because the employer strongly believes that "those people are all lazy." Had the employer hired the immigrant, he might have actually turned out to be the ideal worker. This is called, more specifically, an *attribution bias*, and is defined as attributing specific traits to people with no evidence that this is accurate or true.

I think unconscious bias is one of the hardest things to get at.

—Ruth Bader Ginsburg

Let's conclude our examination of rhetoric with a few puzzles that test your ability to decode hidden meanings in words and language generally. As abstract as this activity might seem, it shows how decoding language is a key critical-thinking skill.

1. If 10 cats can kill 10 rats in 10 minutes, how long will it take 100 cats to kill 100 rats?

2. It takes my brother two minutes to boil one egg. How long will it take him to boil 10 eggs?

3. In one field there are three and seven-ninths haystacks. In another, there are two and two-thirds haystacks. How many haystacks are there when we put them all together?

Key Takeaways: CHAPTER 3

Rhetoric is . . . discovering the possible means of persuasion in reference to any subject whatever.

—Aristotle

Let's sum up the main points to take away from this chapter.

1. Rhetorical devices are used in everyday conversations, for good and for bad.

2. Many fallacies are driven by language. We should always be wary of them, since they occur so frequently.

3. Overcoming ingrained beliefs is difficult to do; using rhetorical analysis can help us deconstruct the language that sustains them.

4. We must always check to see if we ourselves espouse any behavioral or cognitive biases. As critical thinkers, we should always be willing to admit our own faults.

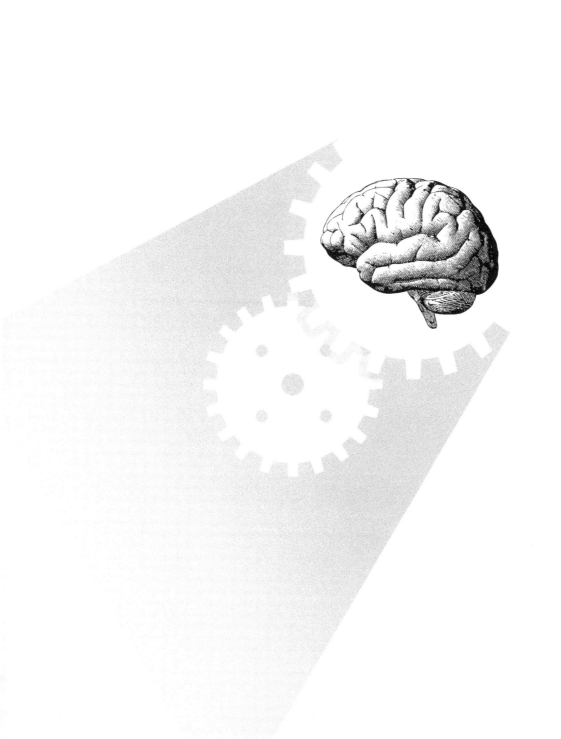

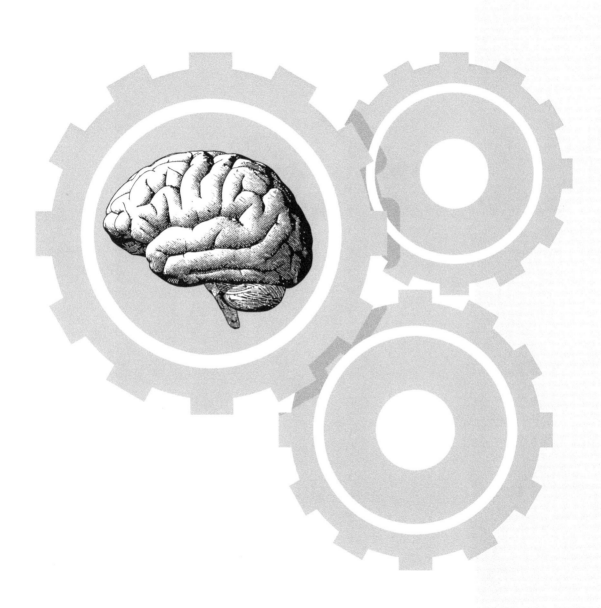

CHAPTER 4

Thinking Smarter in the Digital Age

Have you ever been shopping online, bought something because of a five-star rating, and then been dissatisfied? From restaurant stars to likes and retweets to video views, ratings seem to rule the world, don't they? In the 2019 movie *Stuber*, an Uber driver is so obsessed with getting a five-star rating that he will do virtually anything to get it. Like that driver, we are all susceptible to the ratings game we now play throughout the internet and social media.

We live in an information age, a digital age, a time of online chatter, social media influencers, memes, viral videos, virtual meetings, chatbots, robocalls, smartphones, spam, streaming services . . . With all the content that's constantly flooding us, at no other time in human history has the ability to critically interpret information been more necessary than right now.

This chapter will equip you to be a critical thinker in the digital age. We're going to explore these topics:

- The relationship between data, information, and knowledge

- The origin and spread of fake news, and how to recognize misinformation

- The tendency to uncritically accept or copy the beliefs and actions of those who have gained social influence online—a phenomenon known as *social proof*

Data, Information, and Knowledge

The terms data and information are often used interchangeably, but this is not correct. *Data* refers to raw, unorganized facts and figures. *Information* is organized data, rendering the data potentially meaningful. And *knowledge* results from interpreting the relevant, meaningful information. Seeking to determine whether information is verified as valid or not is clearly a key critical-thinking skill in an age of fake news, disinformation, and, of course, five-star ratings.

To illustrate the connections among data, information, and knowledge, let's consider how a hypothetical political poll can be set up and carried out to help a certain politician succeed.

Data. First, we prepare a questionnaire and send it out via social media to a selected sample of the target population. The questions require a yes/no response, with follow-up questions: "Would you vote for this candidate? Why or why not?" "Do you think this party represents traditional values? Why or why not?"

Information. We then classify the responses according to specific categories, such as liberal responses, conservative responses, and so on. These can then be further subdivided into the subject's specific take on such things as family values, social policies, religion, economic policy, and so forth. The data, now organized in various ways, will show patterns, especially if we use statistical and visual techniques such as charts, histograms, and diagrams.

Knowledge. Now, armed with the relevant information, we can develop a hypothesis and use it to plan our strategy. What started as raw numbers has become a road map to guide us forward.

Information can always be manipulated for specific self-serving purposes—that is, data can be organized in inaccurate or deceptive ways. To immunize yourself against such manipulation, always observe these warning signs:

Biased polling. When considering the result of any kind of survey, be sure to consider the questions that were asked. Be vigilant about how questions are phrased, and look for language that's likely to elicit a particular response.

> *Example:* Biased language: "Do you believe that immigrants are abusing the system, since they take work away from citizens?"
> Neutral language: "In what ways do you think immigration impacts society?"

Misleading data presentation. Even if the questions are bias-free, the results can always be used for self-serving purposes. Recognizing selection bias is tricky, unless you are an expert, so it's good to look for an analysis that is conducted by a trusted source. Questions to ask include "How was the sample chosen?" and "What criteria were used?" If the answers are deflective or circular, then you have likely detected selection bias.

Data dredging. Also known as data fishing, this is the misuse of data to show patterns in it that appear to be significant but in reality are not. An example is using data about the weather to show climate trends, but selecting data from a very narrow time span or excluding certain years from the sample. As in the case of misleading data presentation, it is difficult to spot clues to data dredging, so always check with expert sources.

———————————

It is a capital mistake to theorize before one has data.

—Sherlock Holmes

RECOGNITION ABOVE ALL ELSE

Indicate whether each of these statements belongs in the category of data, information, or knowledge.

1. "In 1918, the so-called Spanish flu pandemic affected one-third of the world's population at the time and killed an estimated 50 million people."

2. "There were no effective drugs or treatments for this strain of the flu at the time. So based on the advice of medical practitioners, it was recommended that people wear masks and that places where people congregated in great numbers be shut down for a while."

3. "The Spanish flu was first observed in Europe, North America, and areas of Asia before it spread to almost every other part of the world in just a few months. The compiled data had made it possible to anticipate this spread in advance."

BEWARE OF BIAS!

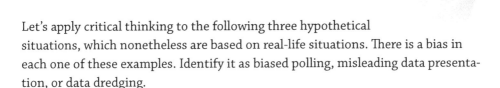

Let's apply critical thinking to the following three hypothetical situations, which nonetheless are based on real-life situations. There is a bias in each one of these examples. Identify it as biased polling, misleading data presentation, or data dredging.

Situation: A report from a reputable source shows up in your social media feed, citing research that indicates that moderate vaping does not cause any harm, especially when compared to smoking cigarettes. A few days later, the same source publishes a retraction of the article, informing readers that they found experts who showed how the data was misused. The new story shows that data was used selectively, excluding cases of significant illness.

Situation: A news and opinion website published charts and statistics that purportedly showed that global warming was stopping or was greatly exaggerated. The graphs were based on air temperatures but ignored other data.

Situation: You open an email poll that arrived in your inbox this morning. The first two questions are "How uninformed do you think Congressman Smith is when it comes to immigration policy?" and "What do you like about Congresswoman Jones's policy views?"

The Era of Fake News

What is *fake news*, besides an accusation used to reject unwanted criticism? By definition, it's news reporting that's made to look authentic but that contains deception or lies.

The first example of fake news in journalism can be traced to 1835, when an article in the *New York Sun* reported that there was life on the moon (see the case study on page 100). Many believed the story to be true, and it gained wide popularity despite the lack of empirical evidence to support the contentions in the story.

Some of the factors that make the current trends in fake news different from earlier forms are the following:

The increased sophistication employed in its production, with up-to-the-minute software and algorithms

The enormous scale on which fake news is being produced

The speed, efficacy, and range with which it is being spread

Fake news comes in two main forms: as *disinformation* or as *misinformation*. The former is false information created and spread to deceive people, while the latter is simply incorrect information.

Disinformation is spread mainly through the internet and can be so realistic and persuasive that it might attract groups of people to websites. The danger is that it will generally promote a particular political, social, or ideological agenda. Sometimes, however, what seems to be fake news may be only satire or parody, which uses disinformation on purpose to amuse users or to emphasize something, rather than to deceive. So, fake news may be distinguished not just by the falsity of its claims, but also by intent and by the audiences to which it is directed.

Fake information exists alongside real information, so we must be extremely cautious about what we read online. Here are nine tips for spotting online fake news:

1. **Beware of clickbait.** If a headline or hashtag doesn't match the content of an article, then it is likely to be fake. This is called *clickbait*, a headline designed to catch your attention so that you will click on the site. The content may be misleading at best and false at worst.

2. **Check the source.** Always be wary of sites with domain names that are not common or that mimic or falsely allude to an authoritative source, such as a legitimate news channel ("cbsnews.com.su" rather than "cbsnews.com," for example). Research the author of the article or report, and investigate any website you're not familiar with.

3. **Be wary of social media sharing.** Just because information is trending on Twitter, popular on Facebook, or prominent on other social media channels, that doesn't mean it's accurate or legitimate. It only means that lots of people are upvoting it. And as we know from the bandwagon fallacy, the popularity of an assertion doesn't mean it's true. Check the same content with a reputable source.

4. **Beware of fake images.** Sophisticated editing software allows fake news perpetrators to make their images look real. You can use reverse image search tools, available on Google and other search engines, to check whether an image has already been debunked. And, again, check multiple credible news sources.

5. **Check reader comments.** If a news item, report, or story is shared broadly on social media, either on the site itself or somewhere in the chain of linkages, you will likely find reader comments on it, which will provide relevant feedback about the validity of the post or news item. If a story shared on social media is misleading or fake, many readers will express their frustrations in the comments section. Needless to say, reader comments may also contain falsehoods and misinformation. But the more we search, and the more consensus on something there is, the more likely that the comments are credible. Still, we should always take everything with a grain of salt.

6. **Check the spelling and grammar.** Many fake news reports are perpetrated by groups who may not know the exact spelling or grammar of the English language. While online literacy rules are rather loose, there are still conventions that are violated unwittingly by the fakesters. If the item has a large number of errors, strange phrasing, or misuse of

common expressions and idioms, be skeptical. Credible news sources have editors who check for errors.

7. **Look for discrepancies with other sites.** Any meaningful information will be covered by multiple sources. If the item in question is in contrast with other sites reporting on the same content, then it is likely a sign that it is fake or at least in error. It's always judicious to consult multiple news sources to assess where the truth is.

8. **Consult a fact-checker.** Alongside the rise of fake news, a number of independent fact-checking outlets will identify something as fake or real. FactCheck.org, Snopes.com, PolitiFact.com, and fact-checking reports by NPR, CNN, ABC, and the *Washington Post* are among the most well-established debunkers.

9. **Beware of recycled stories.** Many fake news articles recycle legitimate headlines, modifying them in content or twisting the facts. Sometimes past events are presented as if they're current and relevant. Often a simple search can reveal whether a story has appeared before or is an alteration of a more credible account.

There is no rest stop on the misinformation highway.

—**Dahlia Lithwick**

CASE STUDY: *RUSSIAN INTERFERENCE IN THE 2016 AMERICAN ELECTION*

Propaganda campaigns in politics go back to antiquity. However, never before the twentieth century did they become so effective—due in large part to the advent of electronic media. US president Franklin D. Roosevelt was one of the first politicians to use radio as a propaganda tool, bypassing the press and directly addressing the American people with his "fireside chats" during the Great Depression. Roosevelt clearly grasped that the emotional power of the voice on the radio would be much more persuasive than any logical argument he might put into print.

In the digital age, social media and other information channels have been used to perpetrate falsehoods and fake news about political candidates to an unprecedented degree. The most robust example may be the Russian-based interference campaign in the American 2016 presidential election, which disseminated seemingly legitimate information via social media channels to reinforce opinions and biases of specific groups. The campaign was operated by a St. Petersburg company called the Internet Research Agency (IRA), which created fake social media accounts to impersonate American interest groups and spread disinformation.

The IRA employed two main strategies. One was to dissuade the Black community from voting for Hillary Clinton, encouraging them to stay away from the voting booths. The second main strategy was to incentivize conservative voters to come out and vote for Donald Trump. We must always be wary of fake news, since it comes in so many cunning disguises, as the Russian campaign showed. It had serious consequences, increasing social discord in the United States.

FIND THE FAKE NEWS

How good are you at spotting signs of counterfeit news reports?
Test your acumen with these scenarios.

1. If the following tweet turned up in your feed, what would tip you off that it's bogus?

   "Did you know that the virus was concocted in a laboratory? Check out our report from an authoritative source: abcnews.com.ty/virus-story."

   _____

   _____

2. Someone forwards you an email with this subject line: *"Federal government to institute martial law next week."* How would you check whether the content is authentic, without clicking the link in the email?

   _____

   _____

3. The following message appears in your news feed: *"Read this shocking investigative report! Your life depends on it!"* What makes it untrustworthy?

   _____

   _____

LEGITIMATE OR NOT?

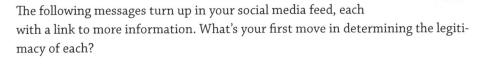

The following messages turn up in your social media feed, each
with a link to more information. What's your first move in determining the legitimacy of each?

1. *"Dr. Jack Kerkid has discovered that a gluten-free diet will extend your life span. Check it out!"*

2. *"Govornmant will tak your librty away. Read how!"*

CASE STUDY:
AN EARLY FAKE NEWS STORY

In 1833, Benjamin Henry Day founded the *Sun* (of New York City), a newspaper that established a "penny press" trend in journalism, characterized by sensationalistic reports of crime, celebrities, and unproven feats of science. One of the first examples of fake news is traced to this newspaper—a series of six articles, starting on August 25, 1835, which purported to report on the discovery of life and civilization on the moon by British astronomer John Herschel. Subsequently known as the "Great Moon Hoax," the articles were instrumental in introducing fake news into journalism, with great success. In fact, the newspaper offices were besieged by a horde of people wanting to read more and more about the moon story. Edgar Allan Poe claimed that it plagiarized his own tongue-in-cheek story, "The Unparalleled Adventure of One Hans Pfaall," about a fictitious character named Hans Pfaall who traveled to the moon in a hot-air balloon, finding denizens and living among them for five years.

The *Sun* never retracted the false story, likely because it was profitable and gained the newspaper a large circulation. An unstated principle for fake news perpetrators is that they should never retract anything, but rather should deny or ignore all evidence to the contrary. What the episode showed for the first time in journalistic history is that people enjoy fake news, preferring it to bland reports about science and politics. Such news seems to spice up life and make it more interesting, much like gossip does.

The *Sun* ended publication on January 4, 1950, but it left a fake news legacy that has been taken up today by all kinds of tabloids and social media personalities. The lesson to be learned from the *Sun* hoax is a simple one: Be wary of all extravagant claims. Check them out on your own.

Social Proof

Humans have an instinctive tendency to think and act like the majority in their group. As social beings, we're inclined to follow leaders and accept the beliefs of others in order to fit in.

Today, this tendency has a technical name—*social proof*, a term coined by psychologist Robert Cialdini in his widely read 1984 book titled *Influence: The Psychology of Persuasion*. He defines it as the propensity of people to copy others or follow along with what others consider to be important. Social proof suggests that we often assume that other people are more informed or knowledgeable about something than we are. The example of the Russian hacking of the American election is, in part, attributed to this phenomenon: People started assuming that what others believed about a politician was critical to how they should vote.

One familiar example of social proof is the use of a laugh track in television programs, a practice that dates back to radio comedies. Adding prerecorded laughter enhances the perceived humor of a show, influencing viewers to laugh along. Although the practice is less common today, its success showed how people are easily influenced by the behavior of others—even if the behavior is an artifice.

Social proof is an integral part of how social media and various apps and websites function; they promote metrics such as followers, likes, shares, views, and votes to draw more users to popular content. And along with popularity comes credibility: a YouTube video with a million views will be perceived more positively than a video with a lower number of views. The danger here is our willingness to accept the opinions and behaviors of others uncritically. Marketers know this phenomenon well and will enlist influencers—social media users with large numbers of followers—to promote their products. And like the canned laughter of the past, some marketers will seek favorable reviews to be put on websites to tilt social proof in favor of their products.

Why is social proof so effective? There have been various theories put forth to explain it, but one that stands out is that we don't want to be different from others. It also stems from a fear that the people we encounter on Facebook, Instagram, or Twitter are experiencing enjoyment, excitement, or knowledge that we're missing out on (aka FOMO, fear of missing out). Being left out of the group experience feels uncomfortable. As the British philosopher Bertrand Russell eloquently remarked: "Collective fear stimulates herd instinct and tends to produce ferocity toward those who are not regarded as members of the herd."

Although lobbyists and other kinds of influencers existed before the internet, the social media universe has given voice to those who fall outside the traditional spheres of influence. Today's influencers have huge online followings that allow them to impact everything from product popularity to politics, despite not having expertise or advanced knowledge.

In sum, social proof is an ever-broadening phenomenon that requires a large dose of critical thinking to filter its potential deleterious effects.

STARS AND INFLUENCERS

In the digital age, there's no shortage of buying advice. Let's apply critical thinking to two popular sources of advice: product ratings and influencer recommendations.

1. **Star power:** You're an independent filmmaker looking to buy new video editing software for a short film you're planning. You go to a website that you have consulted in the past and find these three reviews. How would you rank them in order of trustworthiness, based on the language used? There are over 100 reviews in total, with an average of 3.5 stars.

    Review 1: Three stars: "Good product, but you must ignore one of its claims, that it is easier to use than Director's Cut 5. It is not."

    Review 2: Five stars: "Great software. It served my purposes and I turned in my project on time. Got an A!"

    Review 3: Four stars: "Nice! Does what it says it does, color correction is great, with only a few glitches if you try to import big files."

Undue influence? Below are recommendations that might be made by online influencers about a new messaging app. For each set, rank the three reviews in order of credibility.

2. **Rave reviews!** Here are three excerpts from the reviews of three influencers. Rank them in order of credibility.

   A) *"I can tell you that this is a great new product. As always, you must take my word for it."*

   B) *"I did some searching around and found that this developer has always produced solid work. This is confirmed somewhat by sales numbers, which I was able to ascertain."*

   C) *"The app is very good, as I was able to confirm myself by trading messages with friends of mine. But you know me, I check out my own impressions with others. So far, so good."*

3. **Bad reviews!** Here are excerpts from three different influencers for the same product. Rank these as well in order of credibility.

   A) *"The app is OK but does not really send messages as quickly as the company says it should."*

   B) *"I wouldn't buy this app, even though it is selling well. In my view, the hype doesn't match the reality, it's the same as a dozen other apps. You might want to consult others before making up your mind."*

   C) *"Don't buy this app; it's awful. Believe me."*

Let's have some fun with logical thinking and its ability to get to the truth. The following brainteaser shows how reasoning can detect lies, a key critical-thinking skill in the digital age.

Five suspects were brought in by the police for questioning yesterday. One of them had stolen several thousand dollars from their company's safe. Here's what each one said under interrogation:

Vanessa: I didn't do it.
Shirley: I didn't do it.
Damien: Shirley is innocent.
Marty: I didn't do it.
Lenny: Vanessa is innocent.

Four of the suspects told the truth. One lied. Can you identify the thief?

Key Takeaways: CHAPTER 4

I was brought up to believe that the only thing worth doing was to add to the sum of accurate information in the world.

—Margaret Mead

Let's sum up the main points to take away from this chapter.

1. Information is raw data that's been organized in a useful way. Always be sure that the knowledge gleaned from the information comes from objective analysis.

2. Be wary about the information derived from a specific set of data. Statistics and charts can always be used for manipulative purposes.

3. Always be sure to check everything presented as being true with the techniques of critical thinking. Above all else, never accept anything at face value.

4. To guard against the effects of social proof, always follow up on any purported advice by checking a trusted source.

5. Always read online messages, reviews, and recommendations with a large dose of skepticism.

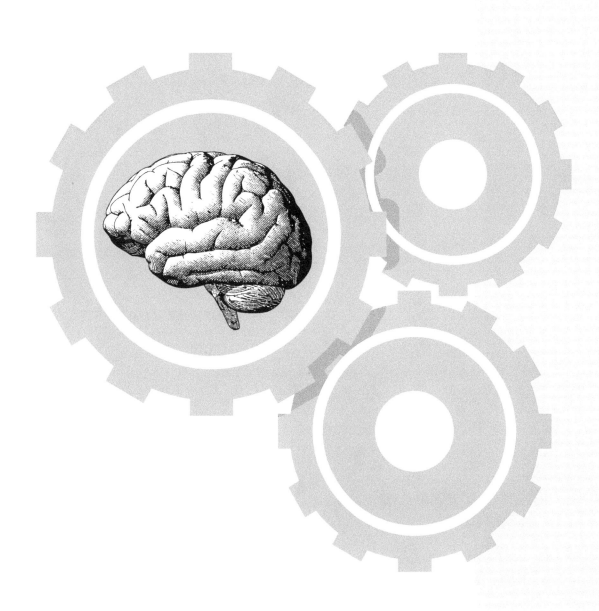

CHAPTER 5

Critical Thinking for Life

Plato once said, "When the mind is thinking, it is talking to itself." The time has come to take your newly sharpened critical-thinking skills and make room for them in your mind, using them every day, letting them talk to you, as Plato phrased it.

One of the most important lessons to be gained by studying critical thinking is that there are two virtues that we all should pursue: humility and patience. The former does not mean a low view of one's own opinions, but rather a respect for the opinions of others. It is actually a sign of inner strength. The latter implies developing an attitude of tolerance toward others, no matter how different they may be from you.

This chapter will cover the following:

- Principles of critical thinking to incorporate into your daily life

- Strategies to make critical thinking a lifelong process

Putting It All Together

To ensure that the skills you've practiced in this book don't dissipate, you'll need a set of strategies to keep critical thinking a part of your daily personal and professional life. Here, then, we have selected seven principles of critical thinking that will come in handy. Follow them, and you'll have the best chance of solving problems, identifying misinformation, and always making the best possible decision.

1. **Identify the problem or the nature of a question.** The problem at hand can generally be allocated to one of the topics we've discussed—the misuse of logical reasoning, the effects of rhetorical language on clear thinking, the clever use of fake news to persuade someone irrationally, or the effects of phenomena such as social proof in influencing one's decisions. Start by establishing the nature of the assertion being made. Is an argument based on ethos, pathos, or logos? Is it even an argument, or is it a nonargument?

2. **Gather all relevant information.** Often assertions and arguments are made without evidence or with evidence that's selected to support the assertion. Ask for supporting evidence and always be sure you have all the relevant facts.

3. **Evaluate the evidence.** Make sure you understand how the raw data was organized, what biases may be present, and what logical fallacies may be at play.

4. **Consider other points of view.** We all have ingrained beliefs and have developed specific opinions about things and about other people. So we must always question our own ideas and actions, considering other points of view even if they stand in contrast with our own. Remember the fallacy of personal incredulity: You should not dismiss anything simply because it seems impossible to you.

5. **Weigh the implications.** Some decisions are trivial. Others, like making a significant expenditure, taking a job, or voting, have significant consequences or implications. You must always weigh these very carefully and take extra care when the stakes are high.

6. **Consider solutions.** Once you have decoded fallacies, biases, rhetorical devices, and deceptive influences like fake news and social proof, consider all alternatives or solutions that make sense. Remember the value of creative, lateral thinking: sometimes an unexpected solution is effective, even if it's not the usual practice.

7. **Make a decision.** The ultimate goal of critical thinking is to enable you to make a decision that's logical and based on evidence and facts, not suppositions, fake beliefs, or fallacies. Once we have weighed all alternatives and used logical reasoning alongside rhetorical analysis, we will be in a much better position to make the right or appropriate decision, even if we do not like it as such.

The important thing is not to stop questioning.
Curiosity has its own reason for existing.

—Albert Einstein

Practice Makes Perfect

Maintaining and expanding your critical-thinking skills is a lifelong process that requires self-motivation and habitual practice. Here are 10 strategies for continuously cultivating a critical-thinking mindset.

1. **Learn something new every day.** To ensure that you keep your brain thinking broadly, seek out new learning experiences, small or large, especially concerning topics unfamiliar to you. Learn a new language, extend your knowledge of mathematics (it can be fun, believe me), learn about new technologies and their implications for social evolution, learn to play an instrument, or learn about other places and cultures. It is not necessary to become proficient, unless you wish to do so. The goal is to keep exposing your brain to new ideas, expanding your knowledge base and exercising your ability to think, learn, and understand.

2. **Solve a problem every day.** I am a creator of all kinds of puzzles that I publish in books and magazines. I have found that this kind of activity makes my own thinking much more flexible and expansive. The lesson I have learned, and which I think applies to critical thinking in general, is that when we are engaged in solving a problem, our cognitive abilities are enhanced gradually. The problem-solving activities you choose can vary according to your taste, from doing Sudoku or crossword puzzles to reading about the ancient paradoxes and how to grasp them. The more variety, the better.

3. **Question everything.** True critical thinking starts by questioning everything, including our own beliefs. When presented with arguments or facts, we should have the five W's—Why? What? Where? When? Who?—as well as How? ready to deploy. These basic interrogatives elicit relevant information that will help us understand an assertion or unravel a fallacy. This is why they are used commonly in police interrogations. Guess who were the originators of this question-based approach? None other than Socrates, Plato, and Aristotle, our guides throughout the landscape of critical thinking.

4. **Become a great listener.** The sign that someone is a true critical thinker is humility—the ability to downplay one's own ideas and to listen carefully and with an open mind to others before making any decision or forming an opinion about someone or something. The ancient Greek goddess Aidos was the goddess of shyness and humility. She was assigned the task of restraining human beings from doing wrong. Her advice is still valid today: When we're humble and willing to listen to someone, we stand a better chance of truly learning.

5. **Participate in group discussions.** Group discussions can occur in all kinds of spheres, from the literary and artistic to the political and philosophical. Sharing opinions with others, rather than insisting on strictly personal interpretations, can only enhance critical thinking. Book clubs are a great place to start (including online communities like Goodreads).

6. **Formulate opinions.** We all need to form opinions. These should be formulated logically, truthfully, and honestly. They should be based on verifiable facts and information. Avoid falling prey to such unconscious processes as cognitive bias (interpreting contrastive evidence according to ingrained beliefs), confirmation bias (the temptation to interpret new evidence as confirmation of your own opinions or biases, whether it is or not), social proof (imitating others because you believe that otherwise you will be left out), and all the other pitfalls discussed in previous chapters.

7. **Be respectful.** It's not always easy to be civil with those who hold opinions we disagree with. But critical thinking has no place for insults, condescension, vulgar language, or hostility. Concluding that someone's logic is invalid, or that they're perpetuating fake news, is not an excuse for an ad hominem attack or verbal abuse. Always use correct, clean, polite, and honest language. This will ennoble you in the eyes of others and allow you to avoid the many linguistic pitfalls discussed previously.

8. **Be vigilant.** Logical fallacies and fake reasoning are everywhere. You can never let your guard down, because the temptation to gain advantage or acceptance by engaging in falsehoods or misrepresentation can be hard for people to resist. Beware of the many danger signs, including arguments based on the straw fallacy and circular reasoning, and the many ethos, pathos, and logos appeals that characterize conversations and messages. Be especially vigilant about information that conforms to your own beliefs, to avoid developing a detrimental cognitive or behavioral bias.

9. **Champion the art of logic.** Our current culture doesn't always value being logical (even Mr. Spock was often criticized for it by his emotional human colleagues). But logic and honesty go hand in hand. So, too, do logic and understanding. Practice the art of logic, and by doing so be an ambassador for this practice championed by great thinkers like Aristotle.

10. **Read critically.** Finally, always have a book literally at hand. There is nothing like reading great works of literature, philosophy, science, or other fields—whether an established classic or the fresh creation of a brilliant new thinker—to activate and reinforce your critical-thinking skills. A good book will project you into an internal silent dialogue with the author. It is the kind of dialogue that great thinkers have always engaged in.

Key Takeaways: CHAPTER 5

Think before you speak.
Read before you think.

—Fran Lebowitz

Let's sum up the main points to take away from this chapter.

1. Always practice the seven principles of critical thinking:

   - Identify the problem or question.

   - Gather relevant information.

   - Evaluate the evidence.

   - Be open-minded.

   - Weigh the implications.

   - Consider solutions.

   - Make a decision.

2. Make critical thinking a lifelong process by implementing the following strategies:

   - Learn something new every day.

   - Solve a problem every day.

   - Question everything.

   - Become a great listener.

- Participate in group discussions.

- Formulate opinions.

- Be respectful.

- Be vigilant.

- Champion the art of logic.

- Read critically.

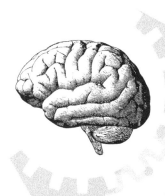

Final Thoughts

Coming to the end of a book is always problematic for me, since it is bound to leave many gaps of knowledge that I cannot possibly fill in the limited space between two covers. My only real hope is that this book has achieved one overarching goal: it has convinced you that being a lifelong critical thinker will help you better navigate everyday situations and challenges. So, as a final piece of advice, I suggest that you go back to the critical-thinking self-assessment quiz in chapter 1 to see how far you have come.

Holden Caulfield, the adolescent protagonist of *The Catcher in the Rye* by J. D. Salinger, made the following observation: "What really knocks me out is a book that, when you're all done reading it, you wish the author that wrote it was a terrific friend of yours and you could call him up on the phone whenever you felt like it." I hope to have been read in precisely that spirit—as the reader's friend.

Learning is not attained by chance,
it must be sought for with ardor and
attended to with diligence.

—Abigail Adams

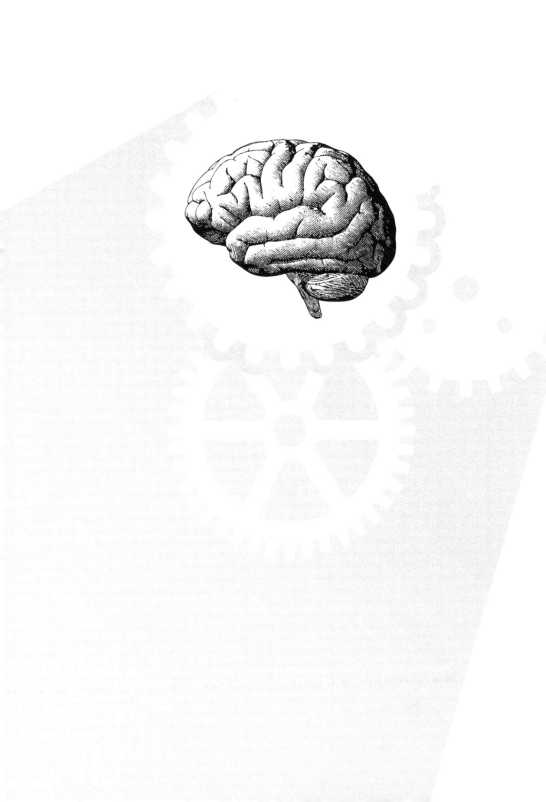

Answer Key

Chapter 1
CRITICAL THINKING: THE BASICS

"MUTILATED CHESSBOARD PROBLEM," PAGE 4

Answer: It is not possible. Why? The opposite-corner squares that you removed are of the same color. With two white or two black squares taken from the board, there won't be an equal number of black and white squares left behind. And each domino must cover one black and one white square. This problem brings out a key feature of critical thinking: recognizing a hidden pattern and how it's embedded in a given situation.

ACTIVATE THOSE CRITICAL-THINKING SKILLS!, PAGE 6

1. **Answer:** If you google reasons for and against drinking coffee, stopping to read and evaluate the information on reputable sites such as WebMD, you will find that scientifically valid research on coffee shows that it lowers depression, boosts memory, and may even lead to a healthier heart. Evaluating the pros and cons of coffee drinking is what should guide you in deciding to drink coffee or not. This is an example of making an informed decision.

2. **Answer:** Before you jump in, you do some research and find out how other popular apps were created, what software and other tools are available, and what skills are necessary. This is an example of considering your options.

3. **Answer:** Much as you'd like to help a friend, it's best to be cautious when money is involved. There are a few things you can do to check whether this is a scam. Is your friend truly in the Caribbean, or might someone have hacked her email account? You can find out by trying to contact your friend by text or phone, or

by asking others who know her. Then, check the URL of that link to see whether it leads to a suspicious website. Also, you might want to go online and do a search for the situation described in the email or even the exact message. You might find that the same scheme has been used on others. This approach is an example of analyzing a situation methodically.

BILLIARD BREAK!, PAGE 8

Answer: First, we divide the six balls into two groups of three each. We can then put one group on one pan of the scale and one on the other pan. That's our first weighing. Since one of the balls weighs less than the others, one of the pans must drop as the other rises. The lighter ball will be on the pan that rises, since that side weighs less.

Next, we discard the three balls that were on the heavier side of the scale. For our second weighing, we put one of the remaining balls on the left side of the scale and another ball on the right. The third remaining ball is put aside.

If the sides of the scale remain even, both balls weigh the same, so the unweighed ball must be the lighter one.

If the scale moves, the side that rises up holds the lighter ball.

How did you do? The correct answer depends on analyzing the information you have to work with: the number and properties of the billiard balls and the possible results of weighing them in different combinations.

A CRITICAL-THINKING SELF-ASSESSMENT QUIZ, PAGE 17

1. **Answer:** You should always opt for C as your default form of reacting to new information (what Dewey called "acting and thinking"). Sometimes, you may have to check more than one source to be sure.

2. **Answer:** Jack is likely suggesting that the cat and dog will be fighting, staying away from each other, and generally not getting along. However, this conclusion is based on a premise that may hold in some assumed general way but might not necessarily be true in this case. This particular cat may be friendly to dogs and vice versa. We must always beware of assuming the validity of drawing conclusions from a weak premise.

3. **Answer:** She's his mother! This is a case of deciphering the language used, analyzing it beyond what it seems to suggest, and then extracting from it the hidden solution. Since the child is not Mary Ann's nephew, and Reuben has no wife or in-laws, that's the only way they can be related. Her apparent lack of concern for her sick child is alarming, but it distracts from the nature of their relation.

4. **Answer:** B. Critical thinkers assess things objectively. When engaged with someone who makes claims without evidence or who hasn't checked the evidence logically, a critical thinker should respond with humility to try to bring that person to the truth. In this case you might say, "Maybe you are right, but would you consider looking at the evidence more closely?" Though there's no reason you couldn't have some cake afterward.

5. **Answer:** B. The only way to analyze it is to conclude that your friend is engaging in what's called the "relativist fallacy," based on the belief that truth is relative to a person or group.

6. **Answer:** A. Even if you are already predisposed to vote against the politician, the information may be fake. So, you could check the validity of the email address, examine the language more closely to see whether it is rhetorically persuasive but factually wrong, and check legitimate sources to confirm the validity of the information. But it's an attitude of skepticism that prompts you to take those actions.

7. **Answer:** D. All the responses exemplify key traits of the critical thinker: curiosity, seeking relevant information, and making decisions based on evidence.

8. **Answer:** C. A key trait of critical thinking is perseverance (B), but another one is to make an informed decision, which includes evaluating the ideas of others to glean possible insights from them.

9. **Answer:** C. Option D may seem like an analytical approach, but only under controlled scientific conditions, administered by experts, should it be undertaken! Critical thinkers are objective about the limits of their ability to gather information.

10. **Answer:** Careful analysis of all the possible combinations in this puzzle will reveal that it's crucial to make the right decision for the first trip across. If the farmer starts with the wolf, then the goat will eat the cabbage; if he starts with the cabbage, then the wolf will eat the goat. So, the only safe, logical decision he can make is to cross with the goat. The rest follows from that: He drops off the goat and returns; he can pick up either the wolf or the cabbage (either choice will work). Let's go with the cabbage. He crosses and deposits the cabbage, but now he has to go back with the goat, so the cabbage doesn't get eaten. (Did you overlook the possibility that the farmer could bring something back across? A careful reading of the puzzle shows that this isn't precluded!) Back at the original side, he drops off the goat and goes across with the wolf. He drops off the wolf safely with the cabbage and goes back alone. He then takes the goat and crosses, and they all continue safely on their journey.

How did you do? The point of the puzzle shows that critical thinking involves asking key questions such as "What is the problem or the case at hand about?" "What can I conclude rationally from it?" "Are there any false assumptions I'm making (for example, that the farmer can only bring things in one direction)?" These imply the use of analysis, interpretation, inference, explanation, and other critical-thinking skills. Perhaps the question we should be asking is just how big is that cabbage?

Chapter 2

THE ART OF REASONING

CHECK THE CONCLUSION, PAGE 33

1. **Answer:** Driving a Ferrari does not necessarily imply that the driver is rich—the driver could be simply borrowing the car or trying it out for pleasure. This is an example of an assertion based on a belief rather than sound reasoning.

2. **Answer:** Getting to work on time does not necessarily imply that someone is a good worker. Mary might be, but she also might not. In fact, she could be slacking on the job. The major premise here is an assertion based on a popular belief.

3. **Answer:** This is an example of connecting a legitimate fact (cats purr) with a conclusion that may not be true. The premise does not state that there's no other reason for Hazel to purr; cats do so for various reasons.

4. **Answer:** This argument reveals several fallacies—false premise (a family ailment is inescapable), specious cause and effect, and relying on popular belief. Of course, a disease or ailment that occurs often in a family is a warning sign, but genetics alone don't determine the development of a disease. In this case, lifestyle factors and behaviors may have played a role. And what about relatives who didn't have heart attacks?

ASSESS THE ASSERTION, PAGE 34

Answers: 1: B, 2: A, 3: D, 4: C

BEWARE OF PITFALLS, PAGE 35

1. **Response:** Who are the leading scientists? What are their reasons for disputing climate change, and do they have convincing data? This argument appeals to an anonymous source for authority.

2. **Response:** Claiming that something is true because everyone believes so does not make it true. We should assess everyone's trustworthiness based on their actions.

3. **Response:** How do you know that airbags alone are effective enough to keep you safe in a crash? Only if that premise is true does this argument hold water.

4. **Response:** It's a bad idea to draw a conclusion from a single case or example. Being cut off by someone may have nothing to do with the driver's age. Next time it could be an older driver.

5. **Response:** You're making that connection based on your belief, not facts. How do you know that he doesn't need assistance because of injury, mental issues, health problems, or some other reason?

TEST OF TIME, PAGE 37

Answer: Logically, one should choose the clock that doesn't work at all. Why? Instinctively, we might choose the clock that loses a minute per day, arguing that at least we will get an approximation of what time it is when we consult it. But here's the rub. Since it loses a minute per day, that clock falls an hour behind every 60 days. It will take around two years to mark the correct time again (and be one minute behind again by the next day). The stopped clock shows the correct time twice every day—at noon and then again at midnight. It is logically the better one!

This is an example of an argument that's logically valid, but not all that useful in reality. The unspoken premise is that the more often a clock shows the correct time, the more accurate it is. By that measure, a stopped clock is more accurate. But in the real world, the better solution would be to take both clocks in for repair.

IDENTIFY THE FAULTY REASONING, PAGE 41

1. **Analysis:** This is a case of circular reasoning: To say the chef's great and incredible is saying the same thing twice, not making an argument in favor of his ability. Why is he great? Because his cooking tastes excellent, because he has vast knowledge, because he has advanced skills?

2. **Analysis:** To expect a team to have a winning season based on a strategy used in one game is an implicit assumption that the strategy will keep working. This may not be the case.

3. **Analysis:** The speaker's making an explicit assumption that a vegetarian has bad ideas about nutrition, but is that assumption accurate?

4. **Analysis:** This is a value-based assumption, appealing to concerns about safety rather than matters of fact.

LIAR, LIAR!, PAGE 43

Answer: Let's assume that Epimenides spoke the truth. If so, then his statement, being a true one, informs us that he, too, being a Cretan, is a liar. But then how could a liar have spoken the truth? So, we conclude the opposite—he must be a liar. But then this means that his statement is untrue, since he is a Cretan and, thus, a liar. Which means he's not a liar. Which means his statement is true. Which means . . . well, you get the idea.

FUN WITH LOGIC!, PAGE 45

Answer: There are two and only two logical possibilities for the first person: he is either a Truther or a Liar. Let's assume that he is a Truther first. If so, then his answer to the question "Are you a Truther or a Liar?" would be, truthfully, "I am a Truther." If he is a Liar, he would never admit it. So his answer, "Juju," would be translated, again, as "I am a Truther." Either way, the first man's answer must translate to "I am a Truther." That means the second person spoke the truth and is thus a Truther himself. The third one obviously lied. So he is a Liar.

It is not possible to determine whether the first man is a Truther or a Liar without further information.

VALID OR INVALID?, PAGE 49

Answers: 1: Valid, 2: Valid, 3: Invalid

BEWARE OF FAULTY DEDUCTIONS!, PAGE 49

1. **Expected deduction:** I will get a good job. However, real-world employment data, not to mention personal experience, may cast the premise of this argument into doubt.

2. **Expected deduction:** Jerry will develop amnesia. The deduction is valid, but the proof of this startling conclusion depends heavily on the details of the poll. For example, it might be guilty of "biased generalization," drawing a conclusion from a prejudiced sample.

3. **Expected deduction:** The mayor is the cause of the unemployment, having damaged the economy. But the argument doesn't rule out specious cause and effect; more specifically, it uses a type of reasoning called *post hoc ergo propter hoc* (Latin for "after this, therefore because of this"). It assumes that because B followed A, A caused B.

DEDUCTION DILEMMA, PAGE 51

Answer: The software engineer is an only child. Amy has a brother. So, we conclude that she is not the engineer. Now, the engineer also earns the least. Sarah earns more than the analyst. So, she does not earn the least and, thus, is not the engineer, either. Who does that leave for this position? Sharma. Consider again the statement that Sarah earns more than the analyst. This means that she is not the analyst. So, who is she? She is not the engineer, either. So she is the programmer. This leaves Amy as the analyst.

This puzzle highlights how facts are connected to each other logically. If someone is the engineer (premise), then the person must be an only child (minor premise, given to us as fact). Amy has a brother and thus is not an only child (simple conclusion). From this we draw the main conclusion that she cannot be the engineer. And so on.

PROBABLE OR POSSIBLE?, PAGE 54

1. **Reasoning:** Inductive. The drug promises to be effective on the basis of the given sample. But further testing is, of course, required.

2. **Reasoning:** Deductive. Government money is given to your department (major premise); you work on the relevant project (minor premise); therefore you will know if the money is sufficient (conclusion).

3. **Reasoning:** Inductive. The conclusion is based on a pattern of medication use triggering anxiety, which is likely but not certain.

INDUCTION PITFALLS, PAGE 55

1. **Expected induction:** Debbie is allergic to peanuts. This assumes a cause-and-effect situation, but it does so on the basis of induction, that is, observing a pattern and making a prediction about it. More facts and evidence are required to reach a conclusion. Can we rule out some other cause for the sneezing? Could the sneezing be a coincidence? Does a peanut allergy even cause people to sneeze?

2. **Expected induction:** I will not get lung cancer. This is dangerous reasoning, since it is a fact that smoking is harmful to the lungs. It also doesn't consider other potential effects of smoking, like emphysema, asthma, or some other disease. Or the speaker might just be lucky and not get anything, but not necessarily because of genetics.

3. **Expected induction:** Brand X is effective toothpaste. How many dentists were actually interviewed? How carefully was the survey planned and carried out, and who conducted it? Have other surveys found similar results?

PSEUDOSCIENCE, PAGE 58

1. **Red flag:** The word "since" implies that this claim is a known fact. But can crystals really do that?

2. **Red flag:** The word "therefore" makes it sound like a logical argument has been made. But what evidence is there to support the explicit assumption?

3. **Red flag:** The use of "if/then" implies a causal connection. But is there reason to believe this phenomenon isn't a coincidence?

THEORY TESTING, PAGE 59

Answers: 1: D, 2: C, 3: F

"DRAWING OUT PUZZLE," PAGE 61

Answer: Three will do the trick. Why? We cannot assume luck, because then two draws will do the trick, if it is on our side. We must assume the worst-case outcome, to be sure. Let's say we draw out a white ball first. Then, under the worst-case scenario, the next ball we draw will be black, not white. So, we now have a white and a black ball in our hands. The reverse could have happened, of course—a black ball followed by a white one. Either way, we will have a white and a black ball in hand after two draws. What will the third draw produce? The ball could be white and thus will match the white ball we have in hand. It could be black and thus will match the black ball we have in hand. Either way, we are now guaranteed a match—two whites or two blacks.

This puzzle exemplifies the difference between probability and certainty. The probability of matching two balls in two draws is low and will not guarantee the required outcome. So to be certain of the match, we discard probability as an option, analyze the information, consider our options, and set up a hypothetical course of action to achieve the result we want.

Chapter 3
RHETORIC, FALLACY, AND BIAS

IDENTIFY THE STRATEGY, PAGE 71

1. **Answer:** Rhetorical question. This comes from the marvelous poem *Creation*, by a relatively unknown poet, Hladia Porter Stewart (1896–1984). The device allows her to emphasize those things that are inevitable to the human condition. There are no answers to her question, correct (pardon my own rhetorical question)?

2. **Answer:** Climax. This is an excerpt from the 1963 "I Have a Dream" speech by Martin Luther King, Jr. It is a condemnation of the discrimination suffered historically by the Black community.

3. **Answer:** Anticlimax. This is from *The Hitchhiker's Guide to the Galaxy*, the novel by Douglas Adams. What's more anticlimactic than to answer the question of what existence is with a simple number? Maybe it does hide an answer, but maybe not.

4. **Answer:** Jargon. There is no clearer example of how jargon can be used to manipulate minds than the way George Orwell showcases its effects in his terrifying novel *Nineteen Eighty-Four* (published in 1949). The incomprehensible jargon obfuscates the true functions of each ministry.

5. **Answer**: Buzzwords. *The Simpsons*, "The Itchy & Scratchy & Poochie Show."

6. **Answer:** Ellipsis. This is a clear example of ellipsis—avoiding the word "die." It comes from *Dubliners* by James Joyce (1882–1941).

7. **Answer:** Euphemism. This is from *Harry Potter and the Order of the Phoenix*, by J. K. Rowling. It certainly does avoid using a profane word, doesn't it?

8. **Answer:** Hyperbole. This is a line from Shakespeare's *Macbeth*, whereby Macbeth says that not even an ocean can wash away guilt.

WHAT'S INTENDED?, PAGE 72

1. **E:** Buzzword. Fat-free. It is intended to appeal to people seeking to lose weight.

2. **G:** Buzzword. Bigger picture. It could also be jargon used in business circles.

3. **F:** Jargon. Paradigm shift. This is typical jargon as used in academia and other specialized situations. It has also become a buzzword in some cases.

4. **D:** Jargon. Parameters. This is statistical jargon but does appear sporadically as a buzzword.

5. **A:** Buzzword. Move the needle. What's more buzzwordy than this?

6. **B:** Buzzword. Bottom line. This is one of the most overused buzzwords around. It initially was part of business-world jargon, meaning the total of some account.

7. **C:** Buzzword. At the end of the day. This is also one of most overused buzzwords around today. I do not know where it came from.

IDENTIFY THE DECEPTIVE DOZEN, PAGE 81

1. **Answer:** False dilemma

2. **Answer:** Bandwagon fallacy

3. **Answer:** Appeal to authority

4. **Answer:** Slothful induction

5. **Answer:** Correlation fallacy

6. **Answer:** Anecdotal evidence

7. **Answer:** Middle ground fallacy

8. **Answer:** Personal incredulity

9. **Answer:** Burden of proof

10. **Answer:** Texas sharpshooter

11. **Answer:** Hasty generalization

12. **Answer:** Straw man fallacy

IDENTIFY THE STRATEGY, PAGE 83

1. **The strategy:** Ethos. This argument is based in large part on a false appeal to a sense of fairness and equal treatment. An ethos-based counterargument could be that in a fair society, everyone should be treated fairly according to their needs. Thus, it is more humane to ensure that anyone who finds themselves impoverished receives fair assistance.

2. **The strategy:** Pathos. This is an appeal to the emotions around tradition. One could argue the opposite and appeal to pathos by describing the anguish felt by those excluded from marriage because of this tradition.

3. **The strategy:** Logos. This assertion takes the form of a conclusion drawn from a premise, but more information is needed to determine whether it's a valid argument. What's the connection between premise and conclusion? And even if the argument is logically sound, it may not be true. Given the complexity of determining the root causes of crime rates, real logic suggests this is a specious connection.

FUN WITH DECEPTIVE LANGUAGE, PAGE 85

1. One hundred cats will kill 100 rats also in 10 minutes, since the time it takes to kill each rat is the same.

2. It will take him two minutes to boil any number of eggs, if he can fit them in the same pot.

3. One huge haystack. Sorry for this one!

Chapter 4

THINKING SMARTER IN THE DIGITAL AGE

RECOGNITION ABOVE ALL ELSE, PAGE 92

1. **Answer:** Data. We are given raw numbers that have not been analyzed for implications or classified into some medical system.

2. **Answer:** Knowledge. This advice is based on the information gained from medical science, especially since the science had not been able to produce a vaccine.

3. **Answer:** Information. This is an example of how data can be analyzed and turned into useful information—in this case for predictive purposes.

BEWARE OF BIAS!, PAGE 93

1. **Answer:** Data dredging. This warns us to beware of analyzed data, since it can be used for self-serving purposes, presented as statistically significant, even though it may not be. Living in an information age, we are all easily persuaded by raw data. We must be wary when it is presented without relevant statistical analysis.

2. **Answer:** Misleading data presentation. We must always beware of data arranged and packaged to present a certain view. Using presentation devices and styles to make a point with the data does not guarantee that the point is a valid one.

3. **Answer:** Biased polling. There are many kinds of biased questions, but these two are among the most common. The first is called the leading question. It is designed to motivate a negative response. A neutral version might be "What is Congressman Smith's view of immigration policy?" The second one is called the loaded question. It is designed instead to force subjects to answer something in a specific way—in this case, to name something positive. A more appropriate question might be "How would you assess Congresswoman Jones's policy views?"

FIND THE FAKE NEWS, PAGE 98

1. **Answer:** The link is suspicious; at first glance it appears to come from a reputable source, but the ".ty" gives it away as fraudulent. Moreover, we should be wary of claims being "from authoritative sources." Authentic news outlets would rarely say this about themselves.

2. **Answer:** News this significant would surely be reported by major news outlets. A check of trustworthy news sources, as well as consulting an established fact-checker, will quickly establish the authenticity.

3. **Answer:** Always beware of exaggerated claims and hyperbolic language. Legitimate news sources would not use this type of language.

LEGITIMATE OR NOT?, PAGE 99

1. **First move:** Research the source. Who is Dr. Kerkid? What are his credentials?

2. **First move:** A legitimate news source would have checked its spelling before sending out the message. Examine the URL to see whether the link leads to a credible source. You could also do a search on the misspelled message to see whether it's been debunked.

STARS AND INFLUENCERS, PAGE 102

1. **Answer:** Ranking order: Review 1 (most trustworthy) to Review 2 (less trustworthy but still positive) to Review 3 (least trustworthy). First and foremost, one must always be careful about reviews. That said, it would seem that Review 2 is the least trustworthy because the reviewer simply provides an opinion based on their own particular experience with the product. Review 3 is more trustworthy since it describes the product more objectively, but the use of subjective phrase "Nice!" makes it somewhat personalized. Review 1 is phrased in the most subjective fashion of the three. However, we cannot make a final decision about purchasing the software itself on such evidence. We need to explore the case a little further, perhaps by talking to friends who've used the software, reading detailed reviews published by a source we trust, etc.

2. **Answer:** Order of credibility: B, C, A (most credible to least). Influencer B is the most credible because they looked beyond their own experiences. Influencer C has attempted to confirm their experiences as well, but not as objectively as B. And influencer A simply asks you to accept their word on faith.

3. **Answer:** Probable order of credibility: B, A, C (most credible to least). Influencer B suggests that followers seek further information on their own, showing a good degree of objectivity. Influencer A shows some objectivity, focusing on the function of the app rather than on themselves. Influencer C is the least credible, because the opinion expressed is just subjective.

SPOT THE CULPRIT!, PAGE 104

Answer: Vanessa and Lenny say the same thing in different ways: Vanessa is innocent. Their statements are either both true or both false. They cannot both be false, since we know there was only one false statement uttered in the interrogation. So we can only conclude that they are both true. Shirley and Damien also say the same thing, in different ways, of course: Shirley is innocent. So, their statements are either both true or both false. Again, they cannot both be false, since there was only one false statement in the set. So, they are both true. Thus, the four truth-tellers are Vanessa, Shirley, Damien, and Lenny. This means that Marty is the liar and, contrary to what he says, he's the thief.

Resources

Online

Argumentation and Critical Thinking Tutorial

    humboldt.edu/act/HTML/tests.html

The Center for Critical Thinking Community Online

    criticalthinking.org/pages/center-critical-thinking-community-online/1360

The Critical Thinking Co. – Definitions

    criticalthinking.com/company/articles/critical-thinking-definition.jsp

Critical Thinking in an Online World

    misc.library.ucsb.edu/untangle/jones.html

Critical Thinking Web

    philosophy.hku.hk/think

The Fallacy Files

    fallacyfiles.org

The Foundation for Critical Thinking

    criticalthinking.org

Monash University: Critical Thinking

    monash.edu/rlo/research-writing-assignments/critical-thinking

Books

Allen, Colin, and Michael Hand. *Logic Primer*. Cambridge, MA: MIT Press, 2001.

Black, Max. *Critical Thinking: An Introduction to Logic and Scientific Method*. New York: Prentice-Hall, 1946.

Carroll, Lewis. *The Game of Logic*. 1886. Facsimile of the first edition. New York: Dover, 1958.

Cialdini, Robert B. *Influence: The Psychology of Persuasion*. New York: HarperCollins, 1984.

de Bono, Edward. *Lateral Thinking: Creativity Step by Step*. New York: Harper & Row, 1970.

Dobelli, Rolf. *The Art of Thinking Clearly*. New York: HarperCollins, 2013.

Gibson, Boyce. *Logic: A Very Short Introduction*. Oxford: Oxford University Press, 2000.

Halpern, Diane F. *Thinking Critically about Critical Thinking*. 4th ed. New York: Routledge, 2002.

Heath, Chip, and Dan Heath. *Decisive: How to Make Better Decisions in Life and Work*. New York: Crown Business, 2013.

Kahneman, Daniel. *Thinking, Fast and Slow*. New York: Farrar, Straus & Giroux, 2011.

McKey, Zoe. *Think in Systems*. CreateSpace Independent Publishing Platform, 2018.

Paul, Richard, and Linda Elder. *Critical Thinking: Tools for Taking Charge of Your Professional and Personal Life*. 2nd ed. Englewood Cliffs, NJ: Prentice-Hall, 2014.

Watanabe, Ken. *Problem Solving 101*. London: Penguin, 2009.

Weston, Anthony. *A Rulebook for Arguments*. Indianapolis: Hackett, 2017.

References

Alcuin. *Propositiones ad acuendos iuvenes* (Problems to Sharpen the Young). mathshistory .st-andrews.ac.uk/HistTopics/Alcuin_book.

Adams, Abigail. Letter to John Adams. 8 May 1780. founders.archives.gov.

Adams, Douglas. *The Hitchhiker's Guide to the Galaxy*. London: Penguin, 2014.

Arendt, Hannah. *Critical Essays*. Edited by Lewis P. Hinchman and Sandra K. Hinchman. Albany: State University of New York Press, 1994.

Aristotle. *Poetics*. 350 BCE. Accessed April 27, 2020. classics.mit.edu/Aristotle/poetics.html.

Aristotle. *Prior Analytics*. 350 BCE. Accessed April 29, 2020. classics.mit.edu/Aristotle /prior.html.

Aristotle. *Rhetoric*. 350 BCE. Accessed April 26, 2020. classics.mit.edu/Aristotle/rhetoric.html.

Bacon, Francis. *Essays*. 1597. Reprint: Boston: Little, Brown, 1884.

Baillargeon, Normand. *A Short Course in Intellectual Self-Defense*. New York: Seven Stories Press, 2008.

BBC.com. "Maya Angelou in Her Own Words." 28 May 2014. Accessed April 3, 2020. BBC.com /news/world-us-canada-27610770.

Black, Max. *Critical Thinking: An Introduction to Logic and Scientific Method*. New York: Prentice-Hall, 1946.

Browning, Elizabeth Barrett. "Casa Guidi Windows." 1851. In Elizabeth Barrett Browning, *Selected Writings*, ed. Josie Billington and Philip Davis. Oxford: Oxford University Press, 2014.

Carnegie, Dale. *How to Win Friends and Influence People*. New York: Simon & Schuster, 1936.

Carroll, Lewis. *Alice's Adventures in Wonderland*. London: Macmillan, 1865.

Carroll, Lewis. *A Tangled Tale*. London: Macmillan, 1865.

Carroll, Lewis. *Through the Looking-Glass, and What Alice Found There*. London: Macmillan, 1871.

Chesterton, G. K. *The Napoleon of Notting Hill*. London: Bodley Head, 1904.

Cialdini, Robert B. *Influence: The Psychology of Persuasion*. New York: HarperCollins, 1984.

de Bono, Edward. *Lateral Thinking: Creativity Step by Step*. New York: Harper & Row, 1970.

The Democratic Strategist (blog). "No Rest Stop on the Misinformation Highway." Accessed April 18, 2020. TheDemocratic Strategist.org/2009/04/no_rest_stop_on _the_misinforma.

Dewey, John. *How We Think*. New York: D. C. Heath, 1933.

Dickinson, Emily. "The Brain is Wider Than the Sky." 1896. In *Complete Poems of Emily Dickinson*, ed. Thomas H. Johnson. Boston: Back Bay Books, 1976.

Doyle, Arthur Conan. *A Study in Scarlet*. London: Ward & Lock, 1887.

Dudeney, Henry E. *Amusements in Mathematics*. New York: Dover, 1958.

Einstein, Albert. "Old Man's Advice to Youth: Never Lose a Holy Curiosity." *LIFE Magazine* (2 May 1955), p. 64.

Ford, Henry. "Thinking Is Hardest Work, Therefore Few Engage in It." *San Francisco Chronicle*, April 13, 1928, 24–25.

Gardner, Martin. *My Best Mathematical and Logic Puzzles*. New York: Dover, 1994.

Ginsburg, Ruth Bader. My Own Words. New York: Simon & Schuster, 2018.

Goodman, Matthew. The Sun and the Moon: The Remarkable True Account of Hoaxers, Showmen, Dueling Journalists, and Lunar Man-Bats in Nineteenth-Century New York. New York: Basic Books, 2008.

Health Inclusion (blog). "Eliminating Unconscious Bias." Accessed April 9, 2020. HealthInclusion.com/eliminating -unconscious-bias.

Joyce, James. *Dubliners*. London: Grant Richards, 1914.

King, Martin Luther, Jr. "I Have a Dream." Delivered at the March on Washington for Jobs and Freedom, Washington, D.C., August 28, 1963.

Lassieur, Allison. *Astronaut Mae Jemison*. Minneapolis: Lerner Publications, 2016.

Lebowitz, Fran. "Tips for Teens." In Fran Lebowitz, *Social Studies*. New York: Random House, 1981.

Lithwick, Dahlia. Source of citation: quotefancy.com/quote/1791879/Dahlia -Lithwick-There-is-no-rest-stop-on-the -misinformation-highway.

Loyd, Sam. *Mathematical Puzzles of Sam Loyd*. Edited by Martin Gardner. New York: Dover, 1959.

McGuire, Charles, and Diana Abitz. *The Best Advice Ever for Teachers*. Kansas City: Andrew McMeel, 2001.

Mead, Margaret. "The Great Among Others." *New York Times*, August 9, 1964, 90.

Miller, William. "Death of a Genius." *Life*, May 2, 1955, 61–64.

Murdoch, Iris. "Profile." *The Times*, April 15, 1983.

Orwell, George. *1984*. London: Secker & Warburg, 1949.

Paul, Richard, and Linda Elder. *Critical Thinking: Tools for Taking Charge of Your Professional and Personal Life*. 2nd ed. Englewood Cliffs, NJ: Prentice-Hall, 2014.

Peirce, Charles Sanders. *Collected Papers*. Cambridge: Harvard University Press, 1960.

Phillips, Hubert. *Caliban's Problem Book: Mathematical, Inferential, and Cryptographic Puzzles*. New York: Dover, 1961.

Plato. *Meno*. 380 BCE. Accessed April 29, 2020. classics.mit.edu/Plato/meno.html.

Rowling, J. K. *Harry Potter and the Order of the Phoenix*. Pottermore Publishing, 2003.

Russell, Bertrand. *Unpopular Essays*. London: Routledge, 1950.

Salinger, J. D. *The Catcher in the Rye*. New York: Little, Brown, 1951.

Schulz, Charles. *The Peanuts Treasury*. New York: Holt, Rinehart & Winston, 1968.

Shakespeare, William. *Julius Caesar*. 1599. Accessed April 4, 2020. Archive.org/details /stragooshakhakespearesrich/page/n6 /mode/2up.

Shakespeare, William. *Macbeth*. 1606. Accessed July 9, 2020. Archive.org/details /isbn_9780764131400/mode/2up.

The Simpsons. Season 8, episode 14, "The Itchy & Scratchy & Poochie Show." February 9, 1997.

Sontag, Susan. *Illness as Metaphor*. New York: Farrar, Straus & Giroux, 1978.

Spencer, Herbert. *Social Statics: Or, The Conditions Essential to Human Happiness*. New York: D. Appleton, 1866.

Stewart, Hladia Porter. "Creation." Cited in BrainyFigures.blogspot.com/p /hypophora.html.

Tutu, Desmond. "The Second Nelson Mandela Annual Lecture." Nelson Mandela Foundation, Johannesburg, South Africa. November 23, 2004.

Twain, Mark. *Following the Equator: A Journey Around the World*. Sun Times Media Group, originally 1897.

Index

Acknowledgments

I wish to thank Lori Tenny of Callisto Media for her many key suggestions and all her help during the writing of this book. I also wish to express my gratitude to Joe Cho of Callisto Media for approaching me to write this book in the first place. I also take this opportunity to express my deep gratitude to the many students I have taught over the years for constantly inspiring me to think critically. Anytime I digressed with illogical statements in class, they would always bring me back on track. Finally, I must thank my lifelong companion, Lucia, for putting up with my grumpiness as I wrote this book. She makes every day purposeful. Thank you, Lucia.

About the Author

Marcel Danesi, PhD, is full professor of linguistic anthropology and semiotics at the University of Toronto. He has published extensively in the fields of puzzles, language, and culture. He also writes a blog for *Psychology Today*.

CPSIA information can be obtained
at www.ICGtesting.com
Printed in the USA
JSHW012202210820
7403JS00001B/2